As one of the world's l... ...stablished
...an l... ...el brands,
Th... ...in travel.

...ars our
...ecrets
...orld,
...th of
...vel.

... Thomas Cook as your
...ng companion on your next trip
and benefit from our unique heritage.

Thomas Cook **pocket** guides

CORK

Your travelling companion since 1873

Thomas Cook

Written by Sean Sheehan
Updated by Maeve O'Keefe and Sean Sheehan

Published by Thomas Cook Publishing
A division of Thomas Cook Tour Operations Limited
Company registration no. 3772199 England
The Thomas Cook Business Park, Unit 9, Coningsby Road,
Peterborough PE3 8SB, United Kingdom
Email: books@thomascook.com, Tel: + 44 (0) 1733 416477
www.thomascookpublishing.com

Produced by Cambridge Publishing Management Limited
Burr Elm Court, Main Street, Caldecote CB23 7NU
www.cambridgepm.co.uk

ISBN: 978-1-84848-352-1

© 2007, 2009 Thomas Cook Publishing
This third edition © 2011
Text © Thomas Cook Publishing,
Maps © Thomas Cook Publishing/PCGraphics (UK) Limited
Ordnance Survey Ireland Permit No. 8709
© Ordnance Survey Ireland/Government of Ireland.
Transport map © Communicarta Limited

osi Ordnance Survey *Ireland*

Series Editor: Karen Beaulah
Production/DTP: Steven Collins

Printed and bound in Spain by GraphyCems

Cover photography © david sanger photography/Alamy

CONTENTS

SYMBOLS KEY

The following symbols are used throughout this book:

@ address ☏ telephone ⓦ website address ⓔ email ⓛ opening times ⓝ public transport connections ⓘ important

The following symbols are used on the maps:

𝒊	information office	▪	point of interest
✈	airport	O	city
➕	hospital	O	large town
🛡	police station	○	small town
🚌	bus station	—	main road
🚆	railway station	—	minor road
✝	cathedral	—	railway
❶	numbers denote featured cafés & restaurants		

Hotels and restaurants are graded by approximate price as follows:
£ budget price ££ mid-range price £££ expensive

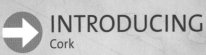

INTRODUCING
Cork

Introduction

Tucked away in the far southwest of Ireland, Cork – fittingly, given its name – is a buoyant city, the second largest (next to Dublin) in the Republic. Kept afloat on a heady mixture of modernity and tradition, it is also anchored by a keenly felt sense of identity and independence. This gives the city a kind of Jekyll and Hyde character: there is a veneer of cutting-edge style to the city – cappuccinos in oversized cups, champagne cocktails in cafés, steel-and-glass constructs, spas on street corners; but behind all this is the gentle pulse of the surrounding countryside and an easy-going friendliness that refreshingly undermines any suspicion of the superficial. Don't worry, though: there is no monster lurking behind the civilised. Cork is very much a community, a place where people have the time to chat aimlessly and the patience to sup a pint while listening to the ticking of the pub clock. A menu might impress with saffron-flavoured, fondant or dauphinoise potatoes, but behind the fancy-sounding names of these dishes lie good old spuds from Cork county.

Cork is an accommodating city and it took the recent decade or so of prosperity in its stride, just as it endured decades of poverty and deprivation in the not-too-distant past; it does not try to hide the division between the city's working-class north and the more affluent south. Rival sporting clubs also divide the city, but the colours you will see most often are the red and white jerseys of Cork's hurling team, 'Come on, ye rebels' being the rallying cry. The reputation for having a rebellious streak is one that is worn with pride by many Cork citizens, and it sums up the confidence and gaiety that make the city such an appealing place.

🔺 *Colourful houses under the church tower in Shandon*

When to go

Cork can be enjoyed at any time of the year and there are advantages to being there between November and late March when visitor numbers are at their lowest. It will be cold but not freezing, dusk comes early and there may be some rain; on the other hand, fine days can also come along, you will have the attractions to yourself and warm fires to snuggle up to at night. Spring brings longer days, visitor numbers are relatively low and the city's green areas are at their most attractive. The summer months can be expected to bring days of sunshine as well as crowds to the city and the cultural calendar fills with events. Long days continue through autumn, and the month of October is a popular time to be in Cork because of the film and jazz festivals.

◆ *The Frames play Cork*

SEASONS & CLIMATE

Cork's climate is a mild one and for much of the summer months, June to August, temperatures average between 15° and 20°C (59° and 68°F). Winter temperatures range between 5° and 10°C (41° and 50°F) and, while January and February are the coldest months, heavy frost is uncommon and snow is rare. These are the generalisations; in practice, be prepared for a day or two of rain or unseasonably warm weather at any time of the year. July and August are the busiest months in terms of visitor numbers and a trip to Cork in early spring, late autumn or in the depths of winter has a lot to recommend it.

ANNUAL EVENTS

March

St Patrick's Day (17 March) There's a grand parade down Patrick Street as well as a general air of festivity in the bars and clubs. On a day when everybody on the planet seems to become temporarily Irish, this is a fabulous chance to catch some authentic celebrations.

April & May

International Choral Festival A tonsil-tingler that has graced the city for many a year, with performances staged at different venues across Cork. ⓦ www.corkchoral.ie

June

Cork Midsummer Festival This feast of dance, music, theatre and literature usually kicks off in the middle of the month. Events can be booked online, where you can also check out the exact dates (which tend not to be finalised until the very last moment). Ⓦ www.corkmidsummer.com

June & July
West Cork Chamber Music Festival Bantry House provides an appropriately exquisite setting for this highly regarded festival. Ⓦ www.westcorkmusic.ie

July
Kinsale Arts Week Held, not surprisingly, in the harbour town of Kinsale, this is a mid-month, nine-day culturaloppalooza (mainly music, theatre, literature and the visual arts) that offers high-quality events in a dreamy environment. Ⓦ www.kinsaleartsweek.com

October
Cork Folk Festival It's sponsored by a brewery, which is appropriate enough given that so many events take place in pubs. There are concerts, sessions, lectures, a pub trail and street entertainment; and the festival usually kicks off with a band playing in Patrick Street. It's light on the chunky-knit jerseys and wonderfully heavy on the good times; it's also an eye-opener for those who assumed that *Riverdance* represents the peak of Irish cultural achievement. The festival usually takes place in the first week of the month, but do check the website for details. Ⓦ www.corkfolkfestival.com
Cork International Film Festival An eclectic mix of films is on offer at this high-profile cinematic gathering (see page 12). Ⓦ www.corkfilmfest.org

Cork Jazz Festival Live bands from Ireland and abroad perform in a variety of venues (see page 12). Ⓦ www.corkjazzfestival.com

Kinsale Fringe Jazz Festival This jazzboree is a chance to catch up-and-coming and niche acts (see page 12). Ⓦ http://kinsale.ie

Kinsale Gourmet Festival The oldest and most prestigious food-fest in Ireland capitalises on Kinsale's seafood possibilities. Ⓦ www.kinsalerestaurants.com

PUBLIC HOLIDAYS
New Year's Day 1 Jan
St Patrick's Day 17 Mar
Easter Monday 25 Apr 2011; 9 Apr 2012; 1 Apr 2013
May Holiday first Mon in May
June Holiday first Mon in June
August Holiday first Mon in Aug
October Holiday last Mon in Oct
Christmas Day 25 Dec
St Stephen's Day 26 Dec

Good Friday, the Friday before Easter Sunday, is not officially a bank holiday but is often treated as one and it is one of only two days in the year – the other is Christmas Day – when pubs are closed.

A Corking good time

In Cork, the season of mists and mellow fruitfulness (well, October) is also one of flicks and mellow flute-fulness (well, jazz flute).

The **Cork International Film Festival** (ⓦ www.corkfilmfest.org) has been running since 1956 and is an established treat on both national and international levels. The programme is usually wide-ranging and features blockbusters, world cinema, offbeat experimental ventures, independent films, shorts and documentaries. The festival is also an important occasion for the launch of new Irish-produced films; one of the many awards announced at the festival is for the best Cork-based film.

Close on the heels of the film buffs come the jazz addicts, who arrive, goatees bathed in golden autumnal sunshine, for the **Jazz Festival** (ⓦ www.corkjazzfestival.com) later in October. Around 40,000 fans flock to the city, so it pays to have your accommodation sorted out in advance. The festival can claim to have hosted many great names and, with recent episodes featuring nearly a thousand musicians from over 30 countries, you can expect quite some variety and maybe even new genres to dig. Tickets go on sale from the first day in September: all the big draws will be sold out in advance, but there will always be unknown jazz bands – some of which will have mellow flautists – playing in small venues where you can just turn up, fling your beret suavely at the hat stand and get jiggy to the sounds. The **Kinsale Fringe Jazz Festival** (ⓦ http://kinsale.ie), which also takes place in late October, has a more bluesy flavour. Its programme is a packed one and all the main pubs and some of the hotels provide venues for the bands and performers.

Autumn, then, sees a rich cultural harvest in this part of the world. Red-carpet days and blue-note nights add dashes of colour to the season's familiar hues.

🔺 *The whistle and bodhrán: staples of the Irish music scene*

History

Positioned on wet land between two channels of the River Lee (Corcaigh – Cork – means 'marshy place'), Cork started life in the 7th century as a settlement based around an abbey, more or less where St Fin Barre's Cathedral stands today. Its proximity to the sea attracted the attention of the Vikings and Norsemen, and for many years it was attacked periodically. A stronger settlement evolved in the 10th century as the native Celts and the invaders settled down together. In the 12th century, a new invasion led by Norman forces from England gave Cork the strong city walls that survived until a five-day siege by the armies of William of Orange at the end of the 17th century. The city recovered and prospered and the walls were eventually torn down; the marshy land was reclaimed and the heart of the city took shape on an island between the river's two channels.

In the 18th century, export trade in agricultural products, especially butter and pickled meats, turned Cork into Europe's most important transatlantic port. Elegant 18th-century houses, some of which have survived, and fine churches graced the cityscape, but while Cork's sense of pride and independence took root, much of the population lived in wretched slums.

Opposition to British rule over Ireland reached a climax in the years after the 1916 Easter Rising in Dublin and, when the War of Independence began in 1919, the spirit of rebellion made itself keenly felt in Cork. The Black and Tans – notoriously brutal and given licence to cause mayhem and terror – arrived in 1920 to supplement the regular British army. They burnt down a large part of Cork's city centre in December 1920 and murdered the mayor, Thomas MacCurtain. The new mayor was imprisoned as a Republican and died under lock and key as a result of his hunger strike.

From the 1930s to the 1960s, Ireland was generally a poor country and Cork, which changed little, was no exception. However, a new airport opened there in 1961, and this was followed by an official visit from John F Kennedy two years later. Events such as these marked the beginnings of a newborn confidence. The Celtic Tiger was roaring by the 1990s, and Cork began to enjoy an era of prosperity that lasted about a decade. Today, Cork is burgeoning on the outskirts, where large chemical and electronics factories still provide work and new road networks are continually springing up, but the city centre remains a place of narrow streets and church spires. The first decade of the 21st century has seen Cork receive the accolade of being a European Capital of Culture. The city is ready to embrace the possibly shaky future with dash, brio and more than a little irresistible charm.

🔺 *Michael Collins, one of the founders of the modern Irish state*

Lifestyle

Cork is very much a working city and as a visitor you will soon become aware of this. The bus station in Parnell Place serves local as well as national destinations, and at rush hours the place is always packed with people travelling to and from places of employment on the outskirts of the city. Many others travel by car, and tailbacks on the ring roads are a common occurrence. Even at the end of a long period of economic expansion, new enterprises continue to grow and delivery vehicles seem to crowd every pavement. Yet, despite the buzz of commerce and light industry, the centre of Cork takes its time going about its business, and you can stroll fairly empty streets until past 09.30; though by midday the shops and restaurants are hectic and a busy pace is maintained until around 17.30. Then the exodus of workers gets under way and within a couple of hours the traffic has died down. A new mood envelops the city. The work ethic does not have an iron grip on Corkonians, and staying behind late in the office is neither expected by employers nor respected by employees. Evenings and weekends are for pleasure, with pubs and bars remaining the heart and soul of socialising, whatever the time of year. The smoking ban has been accepted and dealt with by increasing the number of outdoor tables, and people of all ages enjoy meeting in bars for a drink or two or indeed for a whole night's carousing.

Growing affluence in 1990s Ireland raised the cost of living, and even now locals are likely to be as shocked as the average overseas visitor at the way prices keep rising. Make no mistake about it, Cork is expensive when it comes to accommodation, eating and drinking, and it is easy to spend more money than you budgeted for. Euro notes can seem to fly out of the purse or wallet if you are not careful, so this guide bears the needs of the cost-conscious visitor in mind as much as possible. Spend wisely but enjoy yourself could be the motto for everyone here, whether resident or visiting.

Meeting friends in one of the many attractive pubs

Culture

For a small city, Cork has an enviable interest in art and culture.
There are museums, galleries, exhibition and arts centres,
theatres, an opera house and an art-house cinema. Music, which
has always been an important part of traditional Irish culture,
can be heard in a variety of pubs and bars, while the importance
of the annual Jazz Festival is a reflection of the city's interest in
20th-century music.

The single most important collection of Irish art outside
of Dublin is to be found at the Crawford Art Gallery (see
pages 62–3). It includes work by the stained-glass artist Harry
Clarke (1889–1931) – packed with medieval-style detail in
brilliant colours – that evokes Ireland's keen sense of the
spiritual. Here too is the noted 1921 painting by Seán Keating,
Men of the South, which depicts a guerrilla band waiting to
ambush British forces in the War of Independence. Men in just
such a force travelled from Cork to Keating's studio in Dublin to
be sketched and photographed there for the painting. Some of
the best art in the city takes the form of temporary exhibitions,
either at the Crawford Gallery or at one of the small art centres
or galleries.

The history of Cork is the focus of the Cork Public Museum
(see page 79) and the Cork Vision Centre (see pages 79–80),
while for specialised aspects of that history there is the Cork
City Gaol (see page 79) and the Cork Butter Museum (see pages
94 and 96). While none of these museums is unmissable, they
do provide valuable background information. The Cork Public
Museum is probably your best bet if time is short.

🔺 *Stained glass by Harry Clarke at the Crawford Art Gallery*

△ *Traditional Irish step dancing*

When it comes to the performing arts there is a variety of venues in the city, and in any one week the available shows could include a celebration of Irish tenors, a musical comedy and a stage production of a Samuel Beckett play. Finding out what is on, where and when, is essential homework if you are going to catch a show or a play that appeals to your interests.

The music scene is a lively one. Although the sound of traditional Irish music can be heard, there is also a vast range of other styles on offer. Why not head along to one of the recognised live music pubs and take pot luck with what is on offer: expect ballads, singer-songwriters, open-mike sessions, trad, jazz, blues, loud rock or mainstream pop. Entrance charges are rare, so for the price of one drink you can sample the sound and move on elsewhere if it is not to your taste.

○ *Find the time to relax and take in the view*

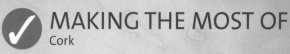

MAKING THE MOST OF
Cork

Shopping

There are plenty of shops in Cork and many are conveniently clustered around Patrick Street (see pages 59 and 62) in pedestrianised and semi-pedestrianised precincts, so it is easy to set off on an extended shopping trip. For a general overview of products and prices you could start in the two main department stores – Brown Thomas and Debenhams are both in Patrick Street – but for something more unusual, and especially for arts and crafts, it is better to seek out individual shops. For Irish music it is worth a stroll up to MacCurtain Street (see pages 58–9). The English Market (see page 58) is probably one place in Cork you should not miss if you're thinking of returning home with some Irish cheeses or honey or some air-sealed smoked salmon.

Handmade craft items make for an original and special gift for yourself or others. Craft studios scattered around the county distribute their products through selected shops and galleries in the city. Ceramics, glass, sculpture, candlework, mosaic and calligraphy all feature, and the range of ceramics is particularly

⬤ *Colourful Irish woollens and tweeds*

CORK CRAFTS

Cork has long been a favourite haunt of artists and alternative types – they were called hippies until quite recently – and the more enterprising ones have established craft workshops specialising in one particular art form. Kinsale is the best place to visit in order to see what is being handcrafted in the county. Pottery is the most popular product, but local crystal and silver are also available and a number of art galleries are testimony to the quality of artists in West Cork. Celtic crosses, sculptures and bas-reliefs made of cast iron or bronze are also widely available. In addition, Kinsale is the place to purchase the black-and-white photography of Giles Norman (see page 107); his evocative images of Irish life and landscapes are highly regarded.

rich, with beautiful smoke-fired pottery and hand-thrown, hand-decorated ware. Forget the stuff on show at the airport shop and the department stores and head for somewhere like Meadows & Byrne (see page 64) off Patrick Street to seek out the giftware and tableware by Stephen Pearce. Cork residents come here to buy wedding presents and the like; the range of terracotta tableware is especially appealing. Dedicated consumers should consider a trip to Kinsale to check out the range of craft shops. Artists have set up their workshops in and around the town, and one pottery enterprise, Crackpots, has a restaurant which serves food on its own handmade plates – you can not only lick the plate clean but buy one just like it to take home.

Eating & drinking

There is no shortage of restaurants offering a variety of cuisines in Cork: Chinese, French, Indian, Italian, Mexican and Thai are all well represented, alongside the more traditional local fare. There is a partiality for Mediterranean-style dishes in the summer and seafood is a big draw in the more expensive establishments. Vegetarians are catered for in two excellent restaurants, one of which is more moderately priced than the other. Most pubs offer food during the day and some serve meals in the evening too.

Drinking is ubiquitous in Cork – it aspires to being an art form – and it is hard to resist spending time in one of the more traditional bars or one of the modern establishments that blurs the line between bar and restaurant. Pleasant outlets for a light meal include eateries in galleries and art centres, and the café in the Crawford Art Gallery is well worth a visit (see pages 62–3).

The only drawback to the enjoyment of eating and drinking in Cork is the generally high cost of living, which is reflected in the price of food and drinks. If your budget is likely to get

PRICE CATEGORIES

In this book the approximate price bands into which meals at restaurants fall are based on the average cost of a three-course evening meal for one person, excluding drinks.

£ under €25   ££ €25–50   £££ over €50

◆ *Plenty of provisions at the English Market*

stretched by eating out twice a day, there are ways of limiting the damage. Weather permitting, picnicking is a cheaper way of enjoying what is on offer locally: both Fitzgerald Park and the green grounds of University College are ideal locations on the west side of the city. In the city centre itself, the tiny Bishop Lucey Park off Grand Parade showcases sculptures by local artists. With a stylish coffee dock at its entrance, it has the advantage of being opposite the English Market. An outstanding choice for picnic provisions, the English Market sells terrific local cheeses, olives, all sorts of fresh bread, delicious pastries, fruit and wine.

In the evening, money can be saved by opting for the early-bird menu that features in many restaurants. This usually involves ordering food within certain hours, 18.00 to 19.00 is common, and choosing from a restricted menu. On the plus side, though, you can enjoy a good three-course meal for €30 or less, as opposed to paying twice that amount later in the evening.

Restaurant etiquette follows Western European norms in most respects, though there is a total ban on smoking in the Republic. For evening meals, reservations are advisable and sometimes essential, especially at weekends and in the more popular places. Similarly some of the more popular eateries will require lunchtime reservations.

Dress codes rarely apply and smart-casual is perfectly acceptable at all Cork restaurants. A tip of 10 per cent or a little more is conventional at most places where food is brought to your table, though this rule does not extend to pubs serving informal meals.

CULINARY CORK

The county of Cork has a reputation for the quality of its food, relying on fresh seafood, locally butchered meat, West Cork cheeses and organic vegetables. The best restaurants benefit from these superb local products and traditional culinary excellence, while at the same time responding to contemporary food trends. A breakfast of scrambled egg with smoked salmon, a light lunch of deep-fried crab toes with chilli and coriander jam and an evening main dish of Cajun-style blackened shark would not be unusual in a county that has been called the food capital of Ireland. Cork also has a local speciality that you might want to sample. It is called *drisheen* and is a form of black pudding, composed of a mixture of pig's blood, salt, milk and breadcrumbs. When it is cooked in a pig's or sheep's intestine, it resembles a small sausage. If you prefer a greener option, try the Paradiso restaurant for the most sophisticated vegetarian cuisine in Ireland.

Early breakfasts can be found in many of the cafés and sandwich bars that have sprung up to solve the one-time dearth of early options. In contrast to continental Europe, dinner is eaten relatively early in Ireland. Early-bird menus start around 18.00, while most restaurants will welcome diners up to about 21.30.

Entertainment & nightlife

Cork is a small city but the entertainment and nightlife scene is not contained within any particular area. The bars and clubs with character and/or live music are dotted around the place, and if you want to experience a few in one night then it's a matter of putting in a small amount of legwork; distances between one good pub and another are too short to require a taxi. The same applies to the theatres and art centres, where evening shows and performances take place.

There is a surprising variety of stage-based entertainment and the Everyman Palace (see page 73) and Savoy theatres are always worth checking out. Opera and ballet performances are available at the Cork Opera House (see page 73), but so too is a great deal more in the form of mainstream drama, musicals and a pleasantly diverse programme of live music events. Occasional performances of classical music take place at St Fin Barre's Cathedral (see page 78).

Bear in mind the closing hours for bars and pubs: from Mondays to Thursdays it is 23.30, on Fridays and Saturdays it is 00.30 and on Sundays 23.00. There is an extra 30 minutes allowed to finish your drink after closing time ('drinking-up time'), and if the Monday is a public holiday then Sunday opening hours are extended to 00.30. For those visiting Cork, or anywhere else in Ireland, over Christmas or Easter, the bad news is that all pubs are closed on Christmas Day and Good Friday; the only way to get around this draconian edict is to be a resident in a hotel with its own bar. Some pubs and clubs – they appear in the After Dark city sections –

have obtained extensions and are allowed to serve drinks until 01.30.

Given that all the venues are located in the city centre, it is probably easiest just to turn up and purchase a ticket for a play, film, gig or special event. Online booking is available for some events, and payment by credit card is usually available on the telephone as well. Tickets for the **Gate Cork City**, the main city-centre cinema, can be booked on the phone (❶ (021) 427 9595) or online at Ⓦ www.corkcinemas.com; prices are around €5.50 for afternoon screenings and €8 at night.

⬤ *The striking entrance of the Everyman Palace Theatre*

🔺 Sometimes it's hard to choose what to see

WHAT'S ON

For current details on nightclubs and weekend events, check the Thursday-night edition of the *Evening Echo*. There is also a free monthly magazine, *Totally Cork*, which has reviews and listings.

The websites below are all worth browsing for entertainment possibilities and current listings.

ⓦ www.corkcinemas.com

ⓦ http://corkgigs.com

ⓦ www.cork-guide.ie

ⓦ www.corkoperahouse.ie

ⓦ www.everymanpalace.com

ⓦ www.savoytheatre.ie

Entrance charges to pubs with live music are sometimes applied, but this is the exception rather than the rule. Clubs, however, are more likely to levy entrance charges. These can vary from night to night as well as between venues – it may be worth phoning in advance to enquire.

It is worth looking at the websites of individual pubs, clubs, theatres and art centres to see what is scheduled for the days when you are in the city. For festival events, see the individual websites. When you are in Cork look out for the noticeboards, plastered with flyers, in places like the Brú Hostel (see page 38), Charlie's in Union Quay (see page 72), the Quay Co-op restaurant (see page 83), Farmgate Café in the English Market (see pages 67 and 69) and the tourist office (see page 135).

Sport & relaxation

SPECTATOR SPORTS
Football
The local team is **Cork City FC** (ⓦ www.corkcityfc.ie) and they play at **Turner's Cross Stadium** (ⓐ Curragh Rd ⓣ (021) 420 2190). ⓘ Tickets and info on upcoming games can be obtained from the **Horseshoe Inn** (ⓐ 10 Curragh Rd ⓣ (021) 496 5044 ⓝ Bus: 3 from Patrick St)

Hurling & Gaelic football
The All Ireland Hurling Championships run from May to September and games usually take place at weekends. **Parc Ui Caoimh** is the county stadium. ⓐ Ballintemple ⓣ (021) 496 3311 ⓦ www. sportsmanager.ie/cake/gaa2/cork ⓝ Bus: 2 from the bus station

HURLING & GAELIC FOOTBALL
Hurling, the game being played in the opening shot of *The Wind that Shakes the Barley*, is played with a flat, baseball-like stick called the hurley and a special ball called the sliotar. The goalposts are like those on a rugby pitch; a point is scored if the ball is hit over the posts, and three points equal a goal.

Gaelic football is played with a ball similar to a regular football but it can be picked from the ground. As with hurling, each team has 15 players and the goalposts are also like those in hurling.

PARTICIPATION SPORTS

Bowling, pool & snooker

Leisureplex Indoor entertainment centre with pool tables, laser and video games and tenpin bowling. Slides and tunnels for children and Friday party nights for 12–15-year-olds. ⓐ 1 MacCurtain St ⓣ (021) 450 5155 ⓦ www.leisureplex.ie ⓐ Buses: 7, 8

Golf

Fota Island Golf Club If heaven has golf courses, they must surely be very much like the three here. Definitely not the sort of establishment where it's a good idea to turn up with six or seven of your grandmother's clubs in a supermarket carrier. ⓐ Fota Island Resort, Carrigtwohill ⓣ (021) 488 3700 ⓦ www.fotaisland.ie

Greyhound racing

Curraheen Park Ten races on the night, bar and the Laurels restaurant (requiring a reservation) overlooking the course. ⓐ Curraheen Rd, Bishopstown ⓣ 1890 269969 ⓛ Doors open: 18.45; first race: 20.00 Thur–Sat

Spa

Escape Many treatments are available here, from massage to rejuvenation therapy and mud applications. ⓐ Morgan St ⓣ (021) 730 6622 ⓦ www.flynnhotels.com

Swimming

Pools open to the public are:
Gus Healy Pool ⓐ Nursery Drive, Douglas ⓣ (021) 429 3073

Leisureworld @ Rossa Ave, Bishopstown ❶ (021) 434 6505
Ⓦ www.leisureworldcork.com
Mardyke Arena A private club, available to the public in summer
(July & Aug). Food is available until 18.00. @ Mardyke Arena, Mardyke
Walk, Western Rd ❶ (021) 490 4751 Ⓦ www.mardykearena.com
Mayfield Sports Complex @ Old Youghal Rd ❶ (021) 450 5284

▲ *Escape to a spa*

Accommodation

There is a good range of accommodation, from country-house-style hotels to hostels, but advance booking is recommended – and especially so during summer months. Shop around and compare rates on the websites of individual establishments with those offered by booking sites such as Ⓦ www.hotel-ireland.com/cork-hotels and Ⓦ www.booking.com or Ⓦ www.goireland.com. The Cork tourist office will book accommodation for you on the spot if you do find yourself in the city with nowhere to stay.

Accommodation – especially in hotels – is expensive, and even an average Bed and Breakfast (B&B) will set you back around €80 for a double room. It is worth considering a private double in a hostel as a way of keeping costs down, especially if you can live without the large breakfast included in the price you pay for a B&B.

Guesthouses and B&Bs tend to be concentrated in two areas: the better-quality places are along Western Road, close to University College, and the less expensive ones along Glanmire Road, near the railway station. All the places below are in or

PRICE CATEGORIES
The ratings below indicate the approximate cost of a room for two people for one night, including tax and breakfast, unless otherwise stated.

£ under €60   ££ €60–110   £££ over €110

close to the city centre, and can be accessed without using public transport unless otherwise stated. From Western Road it is a 10–15-minute walk into the city centre and Bus 8 is also available. When travelling to or from the airport, the Skylink shuttle (see page 48) serves Western Road.

HOTELS, B&BS & SELF CATERING

7 Ferncliff ££ A well-kept and hospitable B&B 1 km (²/₃ mile) north of the centre, with grand views from the family room on the top floor. The other three rooms are doubles. ⓐ 7 Ferncliff, Bellevue Park, St Luke's (Around Cork) ⓣ (021) 450 8963 ⓔ bbferncliff@eircom.net

Hotel Isaacs ££ Characterful Victorian building with self-catering apartments as well as standard and superior rooms and a great restaurant, Greene's (see page 70). ⓐ 48 MacCurtain St (City Centre) ⓣ (021) 450 0011 ⓦ www.isaacs.ie

Redclyffe House ££ All 14 rooms have en-suite bathrooms, tea/coffee-making facilities and private car parking in this family-run guesthouse. ⓐ Western Rd (West of Centre) ⓣ (021) 427 3220 ⓦ www.redclyffe.com

Station View ££ Close to the railway station, 16 rooms, all en-suite. ⓐ 87 Lower Glanmire Rd (City Centre) ⓣ (021) 450 6847

Victoria Hotel ££ James Joyce stayed in this 19th-century hotel as a child with his father. A characterful place, popular with non-

residents for the bar and restaurant. ⓐ Patrick St (City Centre)
ⓣ (021) 427 8788 ⓦ www.thevictoriahotel.com

Blarney Stone ££–£££ Opposite the entrance to Cork University,
eight rooms with good facilities. ⓐ Western Rd (West of Centre)
ⓣ (021) 427 0083 ⓦ www.blarneystoneguesthouse.ie

Crawford House ££–£££ A luxury guesthouse with en-suites that
include hot tubs, it is a ten-minute walk from the city centre.
Self-catering apartments are also available. ⓐ Western Rd
(West of Centre) ⓣ (021) 427 9000
ⓦ www.crawfordguesthouse.com

Garnish House ££–£££ A good choice for a leisurely and
substantial breakfast – try the porridge with Baileys – and a
comfortable atmosphere. ⓐ Western Rd (West of Centre)
ⓣ (021) 427 5111 ⓦ www.garnish.ie

Maryborough Hotel & Spa ££–£££ Perfect getaway retreat
outside the city, an early 18th-century country house with
grounds to wander around, a spa, TechnoGym, good restaurant
and first-rate service. ⓐ Maryborough Hill, Douglas (Around Cork)
ⓣ (021) 436 5555 ⓦ www.maryborough.com ⓒ Closed: 24–26 Dec
ⓝ Bus: 6 from South Mall in Cork, 7 from Patrick St

Victoria Lodge ££–£££ Self-catering apartments using the
university's student accommodation. ⓐ Victoria Cross
(West of Centre) ⓣ (021) 494 1200 and (021) 481 8451
ⓦ www.ucc.ie/campusaccommodation.com ⓛ June–Aug

Jury's Inn £££ Rates are per room for up to three adults or two adults and two children. Breakfast is not included but there is a restaurant. ❷ Anderson's Quay (City Centre)
❶ (021) 494 3000 ❿ www.jurysinns.com ❶ Closed: 24–27 Dec

River Lee Hotel £££ Ultra-modern hotel in a pretty rural setting, within walking distance of the city centre. Huge pool and spa and a comfortable restaurant and bar, with a terrace for alfresco dining and drinking. ❷ Western Rd (West of Centre)
❶ (021) 425 2700 ❿ www.doylecollection.com

HOSTELS

Brú Hostel £ Cork's most fashionable hostel has dorms, four-bed and private two-bed rooms. ❷ 57 MacCurtain St (City Centre)
❶ (021) 455 9667 ❿ www.bruhostel.com

Cork International Youth Hostel £ Large, renovated Victorian house with double and four-bed rooms. ❷ 1 & 2 Redclyffe, Western Rd (West of Centre) ❶ (021) 454 3289
❿ www.corkinternationalhostel.com ❷ Bus: 8 from Patrick St

Kinlay House £ Smart, well-equipped hostel with a range of rooms, including doubles. Breakfast included. ❷ Shandon (Around Cork) ❶ (021) 450 8966 ❿ www.kinlayhouse.ie

Sheila's Budget Accommodation Centre £ A good hostel with laundry, sauna, cinema room and Internet. ❷ 4 Belgrave Place, Wellington Rd (City Centre) ❶ (021) 450 5562
❿ www.sheilashostel.ie

◆ *Brú Hostel*

THE BEST OF CORK

Whether you are on a flying visit to Cork or taking a more leisurely break in Ireland, the city offers some sights and experiences that should not be missed.

TOP 10 ATTRACTIONS

- **Cork City Gaol** Incarcerate yourself in the city's 19th-century prison before breaking out to visit the adjoining Radio Museum (see page 79).

- **Crawford Art Gallery** The most important art gallery outside of the capital is full of surprises and has a neat café to relax in afterwards (see pages 62–3).

- **English Market** Atmospheric, 200-year-old food market selling West Cork cheeses alongside Belgian chocolates. It also has an upstairs café with live piano music (see page 58).

- **Honan Chapel** Stained-glass windows and a mosaic floor in an amazing Hiberno-Romanesque chapel (see page 80).

- **Kissing the Blarney Stone** Get down on your back to kiss the stone and ensure you come away a skilled flatterer (see pages 88–9).

- **Live music in a city-centre bar** This is what Cork is good at: enjoy a pint of the black stuff – not necessarily Guinness – and loud, live music (see page 20).

- **Café Paradiso restaurant** Acclaimed as the best vegetarian restaurant in Ireland and enjoyed by many a carnivore (see page 85).

- **Ring the bells at Shandon** In the tower of Cork's most famous church you're allowed to ring the bells yourself (see page 94).

- **Shopping for local craft products** Take home a treat for yourself or others: for the very best choice, head to Kinsale (see page 106).

- **St Fin Barre's Cathedral** Built in the 19th century, but medieval in its attention to detail (see page 78).

Traditional Irish fare at a farmers' market

Suggested itineraries

HALF-DAY: CORK IN A HURRY

Start with a visit to the English Market (see page 58), then walk through the narrow streets in the St Paul's area and pop into the Crawford Art Gallery (see pages 62–3). Enjoy a light lunch there or in one of the pubs. Later on, head to Jacobs on the Mall for an evening meal (see page 70).

1 DAY: TIME TO SEE A LITTLE MORE

As well as the half-day activities above, a whole day gives you time to visit the beautiful Honan Chapel (see page 80), though you might want to catch a taxi if time is short. Alternatively, walk across the river to Shandon to see the sights.

⬥ Cork City Gaol

2–3 DAYS: TIME TO SEE MUCH MORE

Time to stroll around the city and, in addition to the sights
already mentioned, visit St Fin Barre's Cathedral (see page 78).
Walk northwest to Fitzgerald Park (see page 74) and cross the
river to the City Gaol (see page 79). Make a day of it by taking
the train to Fota Wildlife Park (see page 92) and then on to the
seafront at Cobh (see page 115).

LONGER: ENJOYING CORK TO THE FULL

Go native and take a relaxed approach to the city. Space out
visits to the Top 10 attractions (see pages 40–41), giving yourself
half a day to enjoy the Crawford Art Gallery (see pages 62–3)
and another half-day around the university (see page 78).
Chill out at Boqueria (see page 69) and relax at the waterfall
setting in Greene's (see page 70). Spend at least a day in the
picturesque harbour town of Kinsale (see page 102).

Something for nothing

There's loads you can do in Cork without deflowering your wallet. Some of the best Top 10 attractions are absolutely free: Crawford Art Gallery (see pages 62–3), the English Market (see page 58) and the Honan Chapel (see page 80) are all places you can visit without parting with a single euro. The Cork Vision Centre (see pages 79–80) is also free, and so too are the parks, including Fitzgerald Park, on the western edge of the city and

◔ *Fitzgerald Park*

WALKING THE WALK

This walk starts at the tourist office in Grand Parade. Turn right as you leave it; a short stroll brings you to the entrance of the English Market. If you're planning a picnic later, choose goodies from the range on offer here. Walk through the market, passing the Farmgate Café above you (see pages 67 and 69), and turn left when you exit on the far side. This brings you on to Patrick Street. Turn right to walk towards the river. Turn left at the bridge, on to Lavitt's Quay, and cross the river at the second bridge you come to. This leads up to Shandon, where you can admire the church and the buildings of the Butter Market. Retrace your steps back across the bridge and down North Main Street until you reach Washington Street. Turn right here to walk towards Fitzgerald Park, where you can linger over a picnic and later visit the Cork Public Museum. Return along Washington Street to reach Grand Parade and your starting point.

home to the Cork Public Museum (see page 79), which is free during the week.

Cork is a very walkable city and going by foot avoids spending money on buses or taxis. The attractions in the West of the Centre section are within walking distance and it only costs a few euros to purchase a day return and travel by train to and from Cobh (see pages 115 and 117). Once there you have the bracing sea air, a promenade to stroll along and affordable places to eat.

When it rains

Cork gets its fair share of rain, though it is more likely to be in the form of a soft drizzle or a shower than a downpour lasting hours, so it makes sense to pack an umbrella or a waterproof. On the plus side, there is no shortage of places offering an escape from the rain.

You can stay warm and dry while visiting two of Cork's highlights – the Crawford Art Gallery (see pages 62–3) and the Honan Chapel (see page 80) – although you could get wet walking to the Honan Chapel. Bus No 8 will take you close. Crawford Art Gallery has a pleasant café, so there is no need to leave the place when you get hungry or need a drink. The rain will give you an excuse to visit some of the interesting museums in the city, including the Cork Vision Centre (see pages 79–80), an 18th-century church that has been converted to house a heritage and arts centre. The English Market (see page 58), which is not to be missed whatever the weather, is all indoors and houses eating places as well: the best part of half a day could be spent here without seeing the rainclouds.

Why not take the opportunity to enjoy a little retail therapy? Cork's department stores rub shoulders at the bridge end of Patrick Street alongside the Merchants Quay Shopping Centre (see page 66), home to a range of stores from Marks & Spencer to Holland & Barrett, and to a number of eateries as well. Or spend half a day visiting the working distillery at Midleton (see page 122). A sample of Jameson whiskey will soon warm you up, and there's a restaurant and craft shop on-site as well.

There's no better excuse on a rainy day than to get snuggled up in a bar, and – should you have the stomach and stamina – Charlie's (see page 72) is open from 07.00 every day except Sunday. In winter, an evening in a bar warmed by a coal-and-turf fire with the sound of rain on the windows is hard to beat.

⬤ *Crawford Art Gallery – much more than just shelter from the rain*

On arrival

TIME DIFFERENCE
The Republic of Ireland operates on Greenwich Mean Time (GMT), the same as the UK. During Daylight Saving Time (late March to end October), the clocks are put forward one hour.

ARRIVING
By air
Cork International Airport is 8 km (5 miles) southwest of the city centre and has all the facilities you would expect, including ATMs, car hire, bar and café. ❶ (021) 431 3131 Ⓦ www.corkairport.com

Metered taxis from the airport to the city centre will cost around €15 and are available from outside the Arrivals Hall.

Bus Éireann airport buses depart every 45 minutes from outside the Arrivals Hall and take less than 30 minutes to reach the Parnell Place bus station. The single/return fare is about €4.50/€7.70. Often more useful, though, is the **Skylink** shuttle bus (❶ (021) 432 1020 Ⓦ www.skylinkcork.com) that departs every half-hour from outside Arrivals and stops on Patrick Street, South Mall, MacCurtain Street, Jury's Inn and along Western Road for the B&Bs and guesthouses; single/return fare around €5/€8.

By rail
The city station is a ten-minute walk away from the centre of town, but there is a shuttle bus service that departs from outside the station to the city centre; taxis are also available from outside the station.

By road

Follow the clearly marked signs for the city centre. There are
multi-storey car parks and a disc parking system on the street –
you will need to buy a paper disc from a newsagent and display
it in your car window. The rate is around €2 an hour in the city
centre or for two hours on the streets a little further out, though
still within easy walking distance of the centre.

⬤ *Cork International Airport*

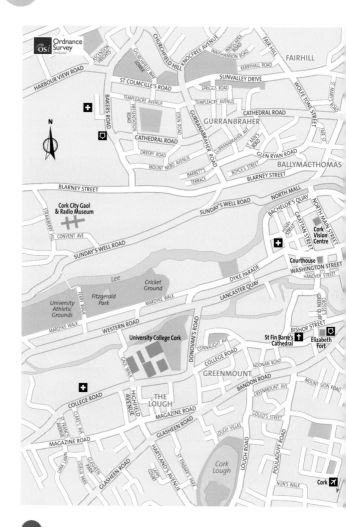

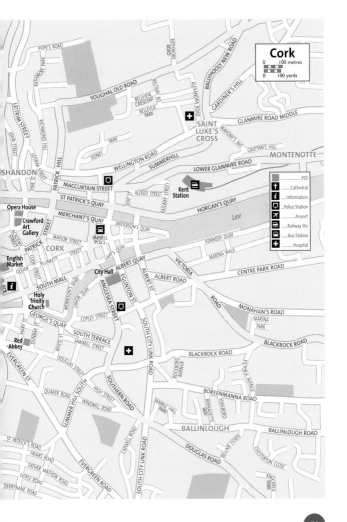

By water
Ringaskiddy port is around 20 km (12 miles) from Cork. For foot passengers there is the Bus Éireann service 223, which runs roughly every 40 minutes into the city. Taxis can be summoned by telephone.

FINDING YOUR FEET
Cork is a fairly easy city to find one's way around, though with two channels of the River Lee flowing through the city there are more bridges than you might expect. Driving is on the left and there are plenty of safe places in which to cross the roads. The pace of life is laid-back and levels of crime are not high, but take sensible precautions: keep wallets and tempting electronic items out of sight and be aware that there may be inebriated youths around pubs and clubs.

ORIENTATION
Patrick Street, the landmark street in the city, is only a couple of minutes on foot from the bus station, where Bus Éireann services arrive from the airport. Officially called St Patrick's Street, though no one calls it this, it curves its way from Patrick's Bridge to a junction with Grand Parade. It is possible to think of Grand Parade as a centre of the city; from here Washington Street runs west towards the university, while semi-pedestrianised Oliver Plunkett Street also runs from here back towards the bus station. South Mall, a mini business district, runs parallel with Oliver Plunkett Street and is close to the southern channel of the River Lee.

Patrick Bridge accesses MacCurtain Street, which runs east towards the railway station. The Shandon area is northwest of

TO THE AIRPORT

The Bus Éireann airport bus departs from the bus station in Parnell Place and you should allow half an hour for the journey. Timetables for the service are available from the travel information office inside the bus station. The Skylink shuttle airport bus (see page 48) may be more useful if departing from a city hotel or one of the B&Bs on Western Road because a pickup service is available if you phone in advance. ❶ (021) 432 1020

the centre and can also be reached by crossing Patrick Bridge. It is very difficult to get lost, especially with a map, though you can get confused crossing the many bridges and the variously named quays. Everyone knows Patrick Street and people are usually helpful in giving directions.

GETTING AROUND

The compactness of Cork facilitates getting around on foot, and bus 8 is most likely the only service you will find yourself using within the city. The service runs westwards along Washington Street for the university and the cluster of accommodation places on Western Road. You can catch it on Patrick Street from outside Debenhams department store. Bus fares are paid to the driver. Taxis (❶ note that licensed ones all clearly display a Taxi sign and are metered) can be hailed on the street and they can always be found outside the bus station in Parnell Place and along Patrick Street. To phone for a taxi, try

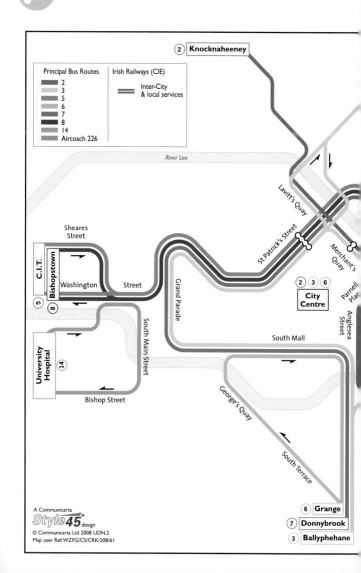

Faranree ③

Mallow & Dublin

⑧ Mayfield & Lotabeg

Ballyvolane
⑦

MacCurtain Street

River Lee

Main Bus Station ㉒㉖

Kent Station
⑤

Littleisland

Glounthaune

Eglington Street

River Lee

River Lee

Fota & Cobh

Cork Airport ㉒㉖

Mahon ②

Cork Taxi Co-op (☎ (021) 427 2222) or **ABC Taxis** (☎ (021) 496 1961).

As far as Out of Town destinations are concerned, **Bus Éireann** (☎ (021) 450 8188) services from Parnell Place will take you to Kinsale, Blarney and Midleton. There are also buses to Cobh, but it is easier and more fun to catch a train from **Kent Station** (☎ (021) 450 6766) on Lower Glanmire Road. The Cork–Cobh train also stops at Fota for Fota House and Gardens (see pages 96–7) and the Wildlife Park (see page 92). Buses tend not to run late at night.

CAR HIRE

A car will not save you time in the city itself, and there are good public transport links to Kinsale, Blarney, Cobh and Midleton, so it is certainly possible to do without. If you want to be more flexible, though, and do decide to hire a car, the best deals are likely to be through your airline website or a car-hire website, with a pickup and drop-off at the airport. Apart from airline websites, check:

ⓦ www.budget.ie
ⓦ www.carhire.ie
ⓦ www.europcar.ie

◗ *The city centre on a summer's day*

 THE CITY OF
Cork

The city centre

The city centre of Cork is its heart, from MacCurtain Street and across Patrick Bridge to Grand Parade at the end of Patrick Street, and it stays mostly between, and always close to, the two channels of the River Lee. This means you are often within sight of one or more of over half a dozen bridges: water, water everywhere – and no shortage of places to drink.

SIGHTS & ATTRACTIONS

English Market

Established in 1788 as a food market – and this is still its raison d'être – the English Market has only recently been 'discovered' as a characterful attraction in its own right. Fresh meat, seafood, fruit and vegetables provide the market's mainstay, but there are also colourful outlets selling olives, local cheeses and coffee and the appealing Farmgate Café, from where you can look down on the market while tucking into cakes and pastries (see also pages 67 and 69). ⓐ Grand Parade ⓛ 08.00–18.00 Mon–Sat, closed Sun

MacCurtain Street

Named after the mayor of the city who was found murdered – almost certainly by the Black and Tans – during the War of Independence in the early 20th century, the street makes an interesting contrast with Patrick Street. Were it not for the traffic fumes and noise, you would be tempted to spend more time appreciating its qualities. There is a good choice of accommodation, pubs, a theatre and some shops that risk becoming cranky in Ireland's mad rush to modernity. The urban architecture of the street is very appealing, but best to visit either early in the morning or after the evening rush hour.

Patrick Street (St Patrick's Street)

Cork's main drag was built in the late 18th century over a curving channel of the River Lee, and its watery origins are still to be seen in what used to be quayside steps leading up to what is now the Le Château pub. This is the only bar and alfresco drinking spot actually on Patrick Street, perhaps in deference to the proselytising Apostle of Temperance, Father Matthew, whose statue stands

⬤ *One of the tempting stalls at the English Market*

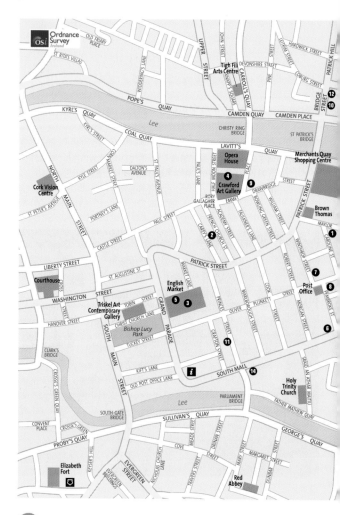

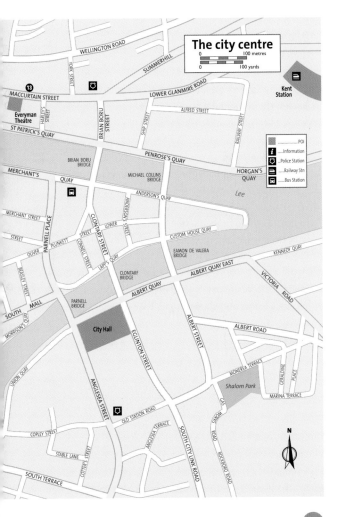

The city centre

| 0 | | 100 metres |
| 0 | | 100 yards |

WELLINGTON ROAD

SUMMERHILL

YORK STREET

13

MACCURTAIN STREET

LOWER GLANMIRE ROAD

Kent
Station

HARLEY'S STREET

Everyman
Theatre

ALFRED STREET

ST PATRICK'S QUAY

BRIAN BORU STREET

SHIP STREET

RAILWAY STREET

PENROSE'S QUAY

BRIAN BORU
BRIDGE

HORGAN'S
QUAY

MERCHANT'S
QUAY

MICHAEL COLLINS
BRIDGE

...............POI

ℹ ......Information

🔯 ......Police Station

🚆 ......Railway Stn

🚌 ......Bus Station

ANDERSON'S QUAY

Lee

MERCHANT STREET

STREET

PARNELL PLACE

CLONTARF STREET

LOWER

CONNELL STREET

ANDERSON'S STREET

CUSTOM HOUSE QUAY

EAMON DE VALERA
BRIDGE

KENNEDY QUAY

OLIVER
PLUNKETT

LAPP'S QUAY

ALBERT QUAY EAST

VICTORIA ROAD

BEASLEY STREET

CLONTARF
BRIDGE

ALBERT QUAY

SOUTH

MALL

ANGLO

PARNELL
BRIDGE

City Hall

EGLINTON STREET

ALBERT STREET

ALBERT ROAD

MORRISON'S QUAY

UNION QUAY

ANGLESEA STREET

MONEREA TERRACE

Shalom Park

GERALDINE PLACE

MARINA TERRACE

🔯

OLD STATION ROAD

ANGLESEA TERRACE

SHALOM ROAD

COPLEY STREET

SOUTH CITY LINK ROAD

BLACKBROOK ROAD

N

STABLE LANE

COTTER'S STREET

SOUTH TERRACE

61

at the top end. Besides the familiar, high-street shops and the city's main department stores, what catch the eye are some bow-fronted 18th-century houses, a couple of delightfully old-fashioned menswear shops and the theatrical street lighting, designed by Catalan architect Beth Galí, which was installed as part of the city's makeover when it became European Capital of Culture in 2005.

Paul Street & around
Go down one of the pedestrianised side streets near the Le Château pub or Waterstone's bookshop and you enter what is rather fancifully called the Huguenot or French Quarter. A number of Huguenots did flee to Cork in the 17th century, and the narrow streets lend themselves to Parisian-style eateries with outdoor tables. The plaza is called Rory Gallagher Place, named after the blues guitarist from Donegal who moved to Cork as a child, and there are some good bookshops as well as pubs, cafés, restaurants and shops.

CULTURE

Crawford Art Gallery
Cork's major art gallery was the city's Customs House for nearly a century from when it was built in 1724. It now houses a permanent collection of Irish art (see page 18) as well as temporary exhibitions of national and international interest. The ground-floor gallery is given over to an eclectic collection of Irish sculptures that spans from classical mythology to Michael Collins. At ground level, too, is a pleasant café (see page 67).

@ Emmet Place **☎** (021) 490 7855 **🔵** www.crawfordartgallery.ie
🕐 10.00–17.00 Mon–Sat (until 20.00 Thur), closed Sun

Tigh Filí Arts Centre You get the full whack of expressive media at this delightful gallery: there's a choice of performance art, sound art, paintings, prints and sculpture. It's not all passive; there are also some great courses available in creative writing and art for both adults and children. If that were not enough, there's poetry reading on Monday evenings – it's amazing what an Irish accent can do for half a dozen lines of doggerel. **@** Cork Arts Theatre, Camden Court, Carroll's Quay **☎** (021) 450 9274 **🔵** www.tighfili.com **🕐** 10.00–17.00, 18.00–22.00 daily

Triskel Art Contemporary Gallery
A variety of contemporary exhibitions and music events with pre-concert suppers is hosted by this progressive arts centre; what you see will depend on the time of your visit. The centre underwent renovation in 2010, reopening in 2011 with an additional art space in Christchurch. **@** 14A Tobin St **☎** (021) 427 2022
🔵 www.triskelart.com **🕐** 10.00–17.00 Tues–Sat, closed Sun & Mon

RETAIL THERAPY

Brown Thomas The oldest and most elegant-looking department store in Cork, this retains an air of exclusiveness with its designer-name concessions and quality merchandise.
@ 18–21 Patrick St **☎** (021) 480 5555 **🔵** www.brownthomas.com
🕐 09.00–19.00 Mon–Wed & Sat, 09.00–20.00 Thur,
09.00–21.00 Fri, 12.00–18.00 Sun

Fran & Jane Party frocks, silver stilettos and designer labels; one of the trendier shops on Oliver Plunkett Street. 🅐 22 Oliver Plunkett St 🕿 (021) 427 9598 🕒 09.30–18.00 Mon–Sat (until 19.45 Fri), closed Sun

Iago Food Co Superb selection of Irish and European farmhouse cheeses – including smoked Gubbeen and West Cork Durrus – plus pastas and continental meats from one of the best outlets in the English Market. 🅐 English Market, Grand Parade 🕿 (021) 427 7047 🕒 09.30–17.00 Mon–Sat, closed Sun

IMB Design Handmade jewellery, lots of designs to choose from and the chance to commission something unique. 🅐 10A Paul St 🕿 (021) 425 1800 🌐 www.imbdesign.com 🕒 10.00–13.30, 14.30–17.30 Mon–Sat, closed Sun

Kilkenny A selection of local jewellery, silverware, bags and pottery. 🅐 Emmet Place 🕿 (021) 422 6703 🌐 www.kilkennyshop.com 🕒 10.00–18.00 Mon–Wed, 10.00–19.00 Thur, 10.00–20.00 Fri, 09.30–18.00 Sat, 12.00–18.00 Sun

Meadows & Byrne Lovely houseware; best buy is probably the local handmade pottery, especially the creamy rich, Stephen Pearce terracotta. Look too for the black-and-white Shanagarry range. 🅐 22 Academy St 🕿 (021) 427 2324 🌐 www.meadowsandbyrne.com 🕒 09.30–18.00 Mon–Sat (until 20.00 Fri), closed Sun

● *Busy Patrick Street hosts plenty of shops*

Merchants Quay Shopping Centre This is the main shopping centre in the city and houses supermarkets, coffee shops, clothes stores and other outlets. ⓐ 1–5 Patrick St ⓣ (021) 427 5466 ⓦ www.merchantsquaycork.com ⓛ 09.00–18.30 Mon–Thur, 09.00–21.00 Fri, 09.00–18.00 Sat, 12.00–18.00 Sun

Pinocchio's Toys & Gifts An array of charming, educational and colourful toys for young and old. ⓐ 2 Paul St ⓣ (021) 427 1877 ⓛ 10.00–17.30 Mon–Sat, closed Sun

Victoria's Antiques This small shop stocks a pretty collection of both antique and reproduction jewellery. ⓐ 2 Oliver Plunkett St ⓣ (021) 427 2752 ⓛ 10.30–17.00 Mon–Sat, closed Sun

TAKING A BREAK

Café Idaho £ ❶ Breakfast includes porridge and waffles. Lunch is from noon and uses local ingredients in dishes such as Cork potato bake and Gubbeen cheese. ⓐ 19 Caroline St (behind Brown Thomas) ⓣ (021) 427 6376 ⓛ 08.30–17.00 Mon–Thur, 08.30–18.00 Fri & Sat, closed Sun

Café Mexicana £ ❷ Traditional Mexican dishes and outdoor tables. Check the daily lunch specials. ⓐ 1 Carey's Lane ⓣ (021) 427 6433 ⓦ www.cafemexicana.net ⓛ 12.00–22.00 daily

Coffee Central £ ❸ This is where the stallholders like to take a break. A good selection of coffee, cakes, chocolate and more.

🅐 English Market, Grand Parade 🕿 (021) 427 1999 🕒 08.30–17.30 Mon–Sat, closed Sun

Crawford Art Gallery Café £ ❹ A small and pleasant café, ideal for breakfast, lunch or afternoon tea, run by Faun Allen of Ballymaloe. 🅐 Emmet Place 🕿 (021) 427 4415 🕒 08.30–16.30 Mon–Fri, 09.30–16.00 Sat, closed Sun

Farmgate Café £ ❺ A great place (see also page 69) for coffee and cakes anytime, breakfast until 10.30 and lunch from midday. Live music at lunchtime. 🅐 English Market, Grand Parade 🕿 (021) 427 8134 🅦 www.farmgate.ie 🕒 09.00–17.00 Mon–Sat, closed Sun

Lafayette's £ ❻ The food is nothing special – sandwiches, salads, hot dishes – but the Art Nouveau interior is stunning and adds everything to a light meal or coffee break. 🅐 Imperial Hotel, South Mall 🕿 (021) 427 4040 🕒 08.00–22.00 Mon–Fri, 10.00–18.00 Sat & Sun

The Long Valley £ ❼ This venerable pub has been serving Cork since 1842. Lunchtimes are famous for the doorstep-sized sandwiches; go early to grab the snug by the entrance. 🅐 Winthrop St 🕿 (021) 427 2144 🕒 11.00–00.30 daily

Peppercorns Café £ ❽ Breakfast, including vegetarian, until midday and then an array of sandwiches and baguettes. 🅐 8 Pembroke St 🕿 (021) 427 1212 🕒 10.00–16.00 Mon–Fri, 10.30–16.00 Sat, closed Sun

🔵 *Modernist street lighting*

FEASTING AT THE FARMGATE
It is hard to beat the Farmgate Café (see also page 67)
for fresh, local food. The oysters come straight off the
ice from O'Connell's fishmongers down below, the duck
is free-range and the beef and lamb are the best Cork
can offer. *Drisheen* (see page 27) and tripe are also
available. You can eat in the self-service gallery area
looking down on the market below, or in the more
formal restaurant.

AFTER DARK

RESTAURANTS

Eastern Tandoori £ ❾ Good-value Indian specials during the week.
🅐 1–2 Emmet Place ☎ (021) 427 2020 🕒 17.00–22.30 Mon–Thur,
17.00–24.00 Fri & Sat, 17.00–23.00 Sun

Boqueria £–££ ❿ A tapas bar with an Irish inflection, so black
pudding and smoked salmon find their way on to the menu.
🅐 6 Bridge St ☎ (021) 455 9049 🌐 www.boqueria.ie 🕒 Bar:
08.30–23.30 Mon–Thur, 08.30–00.30 Fri & Sat, 17.30–23.00 Sun;
breakfast: 09.30–12.00; food until 23.00 Mon–Sat, 22.00 Sun

Ristorante Rossini ££ ⓫ Wooden floors, white tablecloths and
urban-rustic décor in this popular Italian-run restaurant; live
music Tues–Sat. 🅐 33 Princes St ☎ (021) 427 5818 🕒 18.00–23.30
Fri & Sat, 18.00–22.30 Sun–Thur

Star Anise ££ ⑫ Best value are the early dinners, before 19.00, like salmon and smoked haddock fishcake followed by a 170-g (6-oz) beef or swordfish steak. ⓐ 4 Bridge St ⓣ (021) 455 1635 ⓛ 12.30–14.30, 18.00–22.00 Tues–Sat, closed Sun & Mon

Greene's ££–£££ ⑬ Cocktails by the classy waterfall and a three-course set dinner between 18.00 and 19.00, plus barbecues Monday to Saturday during the summer. This long-running establishment holds on to its decent reputation with lots of good food such as Thai chicken soup, roast lamb and turbot with beans. ⓐ Hotel Isaacs, 48 MacCurtain St ⓣ (021) 450 3805 ⓦ www.greenesrestaurant.com ⓛ 18.00–22.00 Mon–Thur, 18.00–22.30 Fri & Sat, 12.30–15.00, 18.00–21.30 Sun & public holidays; breakfast: 07.00–10.00 Mon–Fri, 07.00–10.30 Sat, Sun & public holidays

Jacobs on the Mall £££ ⑭ Check out William Ruane's *Blue Butterfly* painting in this light-filled, sedate restaurant that occupies the site of a 17th-century Turkish bathhouse. Seasonal variations are on offer, plus a diverse wine list. ⓐ 30A South Mall ⓣ (021) 425 1530 ⓦ www.jacobsonthemall.com ⓛ 12.30–14.30, 18.30–22.00 Mon–Sat, closed Sun

BARS, CLUBS & PUBS
An Bodhran A cosy interior, wood everywhere, and the best pub in the city for traditional/folk music. ⓐ 42 Oliver Plunkett St ⓣ (021) 427 4544 ⓛ 12.00–23.30 Mon–Thur, 12.00–00.30 Fri & Sat, 12.00–23.00 Sun

🔺 *Greene's: a peaceful place to eat*

An Brog Very popular with students for its keen prices, eclectic range of music, beautifully painted walls and occasional live music. Gets crowded. ⓐ 74 Oliver Plunkett St ⓣ (021) 427 1392 ⓛ 11.00–23.30 Mon–Thur, 11.00–00.30 Fri & Sat, 11.00–23.00 Sun

Bodega A converted warehouse with whitewashed walls and exposed beams, this bar/club is a popular late-night venue with DJs and occasionally bands. ⓐ Cornmarket St ⓣ (021) 427 3756 ⓦ www.bodegacork.ie ⓛ 20.00–late Wed–Sun, closed Mon & Tues

Charlie's Open at 07.00 and rarely still empty by 07.30, this is a pub with character. Live music most nights and lovely open coal fire. ⓐ 2 Union Quay ⓣ (021) 431 8342 ⓛ 07.00–late Mon–Sat, 12.30–23.00 Sun

City Limits Bar A bit of everything here, from comedy to sports and games nights to DJs. Voted best comedy club in Ireland. ⓐ Coburg St ⓣ (021) 450 1206 ⓦ www.thecomedyclub.ie ⓛ 15.00–late daily

Clancy's Live music or DJs most nights, steak restaurant, and a rooftop garden for smokers. ⓐ 15 Princes St ⓣ (021) 427 6097 ⓦ www.clancys-bar.com ⓛ 10.00–23.00 Mon–Fri, 10.00–00.30 Sat, 12.00–23.00 Sun

Dennehys Don't be put off by the unprepossessing exterior, this is a lovely old bar and the sort of place where you can sometimes just sit and listen to the clock ticking. ⓐ 11 Cornmarket St

☎ (021) 427 2343 🌐 www.dennehyspub.com 🕐 07.00–23.00
Mon–Thur, 07.00–00.30 Fri & Sat, 12.30–23.00 Sun

The Old Oak A lively nightspot that attracts a young crowd.
Live music most nights and a DJ at the weekend. 🅐 113 Oliver
Plunkett St ☎ (021) 427 6165 🕐 12.30–01.30 Mon, 12.00–02.00
Tues–Sat, 13.00–01.00 Sun

Scott's A trendy, lively bar, restaurant and nightclub. With seating
outdoors to enjoy lunch or a latte, this is a great place to people-
watch. 🅐 116 Oliver Plunkett St ☎ (021) 422 2779 🌐 www.scotts.ie
🕐 12.00–01.00 Mon–Sat, closed Sun

Sin E Popular pub with live music – often traditional – upstairs
and comedy nights on Monday. 🅐 8 Coburg St ☎ (021) 450 2266
🕐 10.30–23.30 Mon–Thur, 10.30–00.30 Fri & Sat, 12.30–23.00 Sun

THEATRES
Cork Opera House Musicals, drama, folk music and even opera.
🅐 Emmet Place ☎ (021) 427 0022 🌐 www.corkoperahouse.ie
🕐 Box office: 09.30–19.30 Mon–Sat, closed Sun

Everyman Palace Theatre Victorian-era theatre where a young
Charlie Chaplin once played. Now a lively venue for a rich variety of
entertainment; late-night Fridays are a gas. 🅐 MacCurtain St
☎ (021) 450 1673 🌐 www.everymanpalace.com 🕐 Box office:
09.30–19.30 Mon–Sat, closed Sun; theatre tours: 14.30 Fri; Friday
Night/Saturday Night at the Palace: 23.30 Fri & Sat
🛈 Admission charge

West of the centre

Washington Street, which begins at Grand Parade, heads into the western half of the city and accesses most of the places you may wish to see. Everywhere is reachable on foot, but on a wet or windy day you might want to use the No 8 bus, which runs down Patrick Street – there is a bus stop outside Debenhams department store – and along Western Road to the university.

SIGHTS & ATTRACTIONS

Elizabeth Fort
Over the past year, this formerly ignored 17th-century star-shaped fort has morphed into a visitor attraction. Shops and a weekend market fill its old buildings and central courtyard, with entertainments ranging from jugglers and clowns to historical re-enactments. Christmas sees a skating rink while August hosts a market festival. Enjoy spectacular views of the city at any time or enquire at the tourist office about specific events.
ⓐ Barrack St ⓦ www.elizabethfort.com

Fitzgerald Park
This delightful park, full of superb mature trees, is a lovely place for walking, picnicking and relaxing by the side of the River Lee. Cork Public Museum is at one end (see page 79) and at the far end a gate leads to the river and a suspension bridge, which earns its name as the Shaky Bridge. From the other side of the bridge, it is a short walk to Cork City Gaol (see page 79).
ⓐ Mardyke Walk ⓒ 08.30–dusk daily

North Main Street

This old street, brought inside the city walls in the early 14th century, is the heart of working-class Cork. It has an earthy character that is gradually disappearing as other areas are spruced up and given a facelift. The Cork Vision Centre (see pages 79–80) is here, occupying a late 18th-century church, and the north end of the street leads to the North Gate Bridge – a quick way to reach Shandon Church.

◆ *The Courthouse on Washington Street*

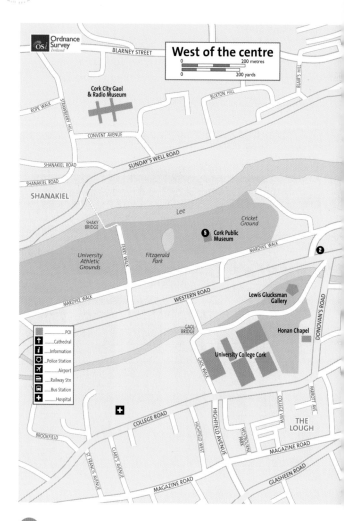

Ordnance Survey Ireland

BLARNEY STREET

West of the centre

0   200 metres
0   200 yards

Cork City Gaol & Radio Museum

BLAIR'S HILL

BUXTON HILL

ROPE WALK

STRAWBERRY HILL

CONVENT AVENUE

SHANAKIEL ROAD

SUNDAY'S WELL ROAD

SHANAKIEL ROAD

SHANAKIEL

Lee

Cricket Ground

SHAKY BRIDGE

5 Cork Public Museum

MARDYKE WALK

2

FERRY WALK

University Athletic Grounds

Fitzgerald Park

MARDYKE WALK

WESTERN ROAD

Lewis Glucksman Gallery

DONOVAN'S ROAD

GAOL BRIDGE

Honan Chapel

University College Cork

GAOL WALK

PARROT AVE

COLLEGE VIEW

- POI
- † ....Cathedral
- *i* ....Information
- ....Police Station
- ✈ ....Airport
- ....Railway Stn
- ....Bus Station
- ✚ ....Hospital

BROOKFIELD

COLLEGE ROAD

HIGHFIELD WEST

HIGHFIELD AVENUE

WESTBOURNE PARK

THE LOUGH

ST FRANCIS AVENUE

CLARE'S AVENUE

MAGAZINE ROAD

GLASHEEN ROAD

MAGAZINE ROAD

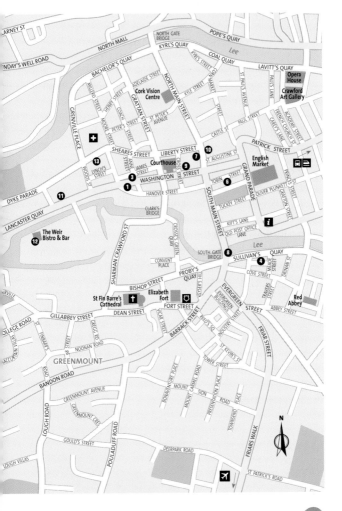

ARNEY ST

NORTH GATE
BRIDGE
POPE'S QUAY

NORTH MALL
KYRL'S QUAY

Lee

'NDAY'S WELL ROAD

BACHELOR'S QUAY
COAL QUAY
LAVITT'S QUAY

KYRL'S STREET
MARKET

ST PAUL'S AVENUE

PAUL STREET

FRENCH CHURCH STREET
ACADEMY STREET
CAREY'S LANE

Opera
House

Crawford
Art Gallery

GRENVILLE PLACE

MILLERD STREET

HENRY STREET

MOORE STREET

PETER'S STREET

ADELAIDE STREET

Cork Vision
Centre

GRATTAN STREET

ST PETER'S
AVENUE

NORTH MAIN STREET

KYLE STREET

CASTLE ST

PATRICK STREET

English
Market

PRINCE'S STREET

SHEARES STREET

LIBERTY STREET

St Augustine

PATRICK'S STREET

OLIVER PLUNKETT STREET

GRAFTON STREET

13

LYNCH'S STREET

WOODS ST

LEWIS ST

JAMES STREET

Courthouse

7
9
CROSS STREET

10

1
3

WASHINGTON   STREET

TOBIN STREET

6

GRAND PARADE

HANOVER STREET

DYKE PARADE

11

LANCASTER QUAY

CLARK'S
BRIDGE

SOUTH MAIN STREET

TUCKEY STREET

KIFT'S LANE

OLD POST OFFICE
LANE

i

Lee

The Weir
Bistro & Bar
12

CROSSES GREEN
QUAY

SHARMAN CRAWFORD ST

CONVENT
PLACE

SOUTH GATE
BRIDGE

8

SULLIVAN'S   QUAY

4

COVE STREET

MARY STREET

GEORGE'S QUAY

DUNBAR ST

PROBY'S
QUAY

KEYSER'S HILL

EVERGREEN   STREET

EVERGREEN
BUILDINGS

TRAVERS STREET

BISHOP STREET

St Fin Barre's
Cathedral

Elizabeth
Fort

FORT STREET

Red
Abbey

ABBEY STREET

GILLABBEY STREET

GREGG RD

DEAN STREET

VICAR STREET

BARRACK STREET

REED'S SQ

FRIAR STREET

IRVILLE

OLLEGE ROAD

FINBARR'S

SYDIA RD

JACCUR CRIN

NOONAN ROAD

GREENMOUNT

BANDON ROAD

GREENMOUNT AVENUE

GREENMOUNT CRES

LOUGH ROAD

POULADUFF ROAD

GOULD'S STREET

LOUGH VILLAS

ST KEVIN'S ST

TOWER STREET

BONAVENTURE PLACE

MOUNT CARMEL ROAD

MOUNT SION
ROAD

PRESENTATION PLACE

TOWNSEND

PLACE

DEERPARK ROAD

FRIARS WALK

ST PATRICK'S ROAD

N

St Fin Barre's Cathedral

The cathedral is associated with the founding site of the city, when St Fin Barre came here from his hermitage in West Cork and established a monastery; the present 19th-century cathedral being built on the same site. William Burges was the English architect and he spared little expense embellishing the interior. The west door is notable, as is the memorial stone to Elizabeth Aldworthy by the pulpit: she was the only woman ever to be initiated into the Freemasons. ⓐ Bishop St ⓣ (021) 496 3387 ⓦ www.cathedral.cork.anglican.org ⓛ 10.00–17.30 Mon–Sat (Apr–Sept); 10.00–12.45, 14.00–17.00 Mon–Sat (Oct–Mar); 12.30–16.30 Sun (June–Aug) ⓘ Admission charge

University College Cork (UCC)

Built in 1849, the impressive Tudor-Gothic quadrangle featured in the film *Chariots of Fire*. If you don't take the tour, you can still wander into the North Wing to see the collection of Ogham Stones – an early form of writing – and enter the Honan Chapel and the Glucksman Gallery (see pages 80 and 81). ⓐ Visitor Centre: North Wing, Western Rd ⓣ (021) 490 1876 ⓦ www.ucc.ie ⓛ 09.00–20.00 Mon–Fri, 09.00–17.00 Sat, 11.00–17.00 Sun (June–Sept); 09.00–17.00 Mon–Sat, closed Sun (Oct–May) ⓘ Admission charge

Washington Street

If you are heading west towards the university grounds or nearby Fitzgerald Park, you will find yourself on this long straight road following the south channel of the Lee: the city end is Washington Street proper, then it becomes Washington Street West, then Lancaster Quay and then Western Road. The

British-era Courthouse dominates the city end of the street, and here too is a string of cafés. As watering holes are harder to find as you head west, this is a good place for a coffee break or lunch.

CULTURE

Cork City Gaol & Radio Museum

Cork's old prison, remarkably well preserved since it closed down in the early 20th century, can be explored with the aid of an audio tape. The finale is a theatrical audiovisual display. The adjoining Radio Museum, in what was the prison governor's residence, focuses on the importance of radio in Ireland and the world. ⓐ Convent Ave, Sunday's Well ⓣ (021) 430 5022 ⓦ www.corkcitygaol.com ⓛ Last admission 1 hour before closing: 09.30–17.00 daily (Mar–Oct); 10.00–17.00 daily (Nov–Feb) ⓝ Bus: 8 to the university, then across Shaky Bridge in Fitzgerald Park, turn right up the hill and left into Convent Ave ❶ Separate admission charges

Cork Public Museum

This museum traces the story of the city's evolution and the historical and archaeological heritage of Cork city and county. There are interesting exhibits from both ancient and modern times. ⓐ Fitzgerald Park, Mardyke ⓣ (021) 427 0679 ⓛ 11.00–13.00, 14.15–17.00 Mon–Fri, 11.00–13.00, 14.15–16.00 Sat, 15.00–17.00 Sun (Apr–Sept); closed Oct–Mar

Cork Vision Centre

Set in the Wren-style St Peter's Church, which was built on the site of a 13th-century church, the centre explores the city's past

◒ *Cork Public Museum*

with the help of a 1:500 scale model and a film on the history and heritage of Cork. ⓐ St Peter's Church, North Main St
ⓣ (021) 427 9925 ⓦ www.corkvisioncentre.com ⓛ 10.00–17.00 Tues–Sat, closed Sun & Mon

Honan Chapel

This tiny chapel in the grounds of University College Cork, built in 1916 in the 19th-century Hiberno-Romanesque style, will astonish you immediately when you step inside its doors. The entire floor surface is covered with a stunning mosaic and your attention is divided between this and the equally eye-catching stained-glass windows, 11 of which are the work of the Irish artist Harry Clarke. ⓐ University College Cork, Western Rd
ⓣ (021) 490 1876 ⓦ http://honan.ucc.ie ⓛ 09.00–17.00 daily (subject to church services)

Lewis Glucksman Gallery

An architecturally distinctive building, with exhibition space and an airy riverside café, dedicated to the full gamut of the visual arts. Check the website to see what is on at the time of your visit, and expect something innovative and imaginative. In summer, there are musical evenings between 18.00 and 20.00 on the last Thursday of the month. ⓐ University College Cork, Western Rd ⓣ (021) 490 1844 ⓦ www.glucksman.org ⓛ 10.00–17.00 Tues–Sat (until 20.00 Thur), 13.00–17.00 Sun, closed Mon

RETAIL THERAPY

Finn's Corner The shopfront cocks a snook at the gentrification taking place all around it, and it makes a pleasant change. Step inside to consider the purchase of a hurling or Gaelic football jersey (Manchester United shirts are also available, of course). ⓐ Corner of Washington St and Grand Parade ⓣ (021) 427 4194 ⓛ 09.00–17.30 Mon–Sat, closed Sun

Mrs Quin's Charity Shop North Main Street has quite a concentration of charity shops, but Mrs Quin's is especially friendly and there is a good choice of second-hand books, clothes and bric-a-brac here. ⓐ 53 North Main St ⓣ (087) 139 4338 ⓦ www.ncbi.ie ⓛ 09.15–17.30 Mon–Sat, closed Sun

Oriental Treasures Come to Ireland and buy something from China... This packed little emporium is filled with products from China – even the Japanese sword is made there. ⓐ 22 Washington St

🕿 (021) 427 9783 🌐 www.orientaltreasures.ie 🕒 10.30–17.30 Mon–Sat, closed Sun

Plugd A good source of non-mainstream rock music and useful notices of up-and-coming gigs in the window. For mainstream music, there is an HMV store in Patrick Street. 🅰 4 Washington St 🕿 (021) 427 6300 🕒 10.30–17.30 Mon–Sat, closed Sun

TAKING A BREAK

Café de la Paix £ ❶ The best all-round café on Washington Street, serving breakfast until midday, lunch – Niçoise salad, tortilla wraps, ciabatta – until 16.00 and an evening menu of gourmet burgers, bruschetta combos and salads. Go for one of the outdoor tables overlooking the River Lee and enjoy a champagne cocktail as the sun goes down. 🅰 16 Washington St 🕿 (021) 427 9556 🌐 http://cafedelapaix.ie 🕒 08.00–late daily (last orders 21.30)

Coffee Station £ ❷ Opposite the gates of University College Cork, this coffee shop is useful for picnic items and lattes to go for lunch in nearby Fitzgerald Park. Paninis, sandwiches, wraps and drinks are available to take out or eat in. 🅰 21A Western Rd 🕿 (021) 427 9108 🕒 09.15–17.00 Mon–Fri, 10.00–16.00 Sat, closed Sun

Petits Fours & Sugar Café £ ❸ Modern-style café on Washington Street serving an array of toasties, wraps and baguettes, plus a breakfast menu. It's busy at lunchtimes but makes for a pleasant stop for a coffee break before or after.

BARRY'S TEA

Barry's tea was once only sold from a shop in Princes Street, from early in the 20th century until the 1960s, and although it is now sold nationwide it remains largely unknown outside of Ireland. In Cork it is recognised as a superior tea and it will be served in any decent café. The tea comes in various grades, but try the Gold Blend for instant and lifelong conversion. Barry's Tea is difficult, but not impossible (Ⓦ www.barrystea.ie), to obtain outside Ireland, and if you are a tea connoisseur it is worth finding room in your luggage for this most discerning brew.

ⓐ 25 Washington St ⓣ (021) 480 6530 ⓛ 08.00–17.30 Mon–Fri, 10.30–17.30 Sat, closed Sun

Quay Co-op £ ❹ Breakfast until midday and then a full menu until closing time: lasagne, pizza, burgers and specials. The self-service food, all vegetarian, changes daily and takeaways are available. ⓐ 24 Sullivan's Quay ⓣ (021) 431 7026
Ⓦ www.quaycoop.com ⓛ 09.00–21.00 Mon–Sat, closed Sun

Riverview Café £ ❺ Situated directly behind Cork Public Museum and part of the same building, the outside tables are inviting for a coffee break; at lunchtimes the indoor tables fill up with office workers. ⓐ Fitzgerald Park ⓣ (021) 427 9573
Ⓦ www.riverviewcafe.ie ⓛ 09.30–17.00 Mon–Fri, 10.30–18.00 Sat & Sun

Triskel Café £ ❻ Tucked down an alleyway, insulated from the noise of traffic, serving breakfast until 11.00 and then a range of sandwiches, panini and toasties, home-made soup, brown bread and scones. ⓐ Tobin St ❶ (021) 427 2022 ❷ 10.00–17.00 or late for events or performances Tues–Sat, closed Sun & Mon

AFTER DARK

RESTAURANTS
Eddie Rockets £–££ ❼ An American-themed diner serving burgers, hot dogs, sandwiches and de-luxe snacks. ⓐ 97–98 South Main

◆ *Continental-style Cork*

St ☎ (021) 427 9969 ⓦ www.eddierockets.ie. ⏱ 11.00–24.00 daily (until 04.00 Fri & Sat)

The Flying Enterprise £–££ ❽ The Captain's Table is the name of the restaurant at the large Flying Enterprise pub and there is a good choice of the standard Irish favourites: lamb, beef, steak. ⓐ South Gate Bridge ☎ (021) 431 1846 ⓦ www.theflyingenterprise.com ⏱ Restaurant: 18.00–22.00 Mon–Sat, 12.00–14.00 Sun; pub: 10.00–23.00 Mon–Thur, 10.00–00.30 Fri & Sat, 12.30–23.00 Sun

Liberty Grill £–££ ❾ This popular restaurant has a pretty dining room and an extensive menu of vaguely Californian cuisine. Service is good and ingredients are, where possible, organic and locally sourced. ⓐ 32 Washington St ☎ (021) 427 1049 ⓦ www.libertygrillcork.com ⏱ 08.00–22.00 Mon–Sat, closed Sun

Wagamama £–££ ❿ The Cork branch of the Japanese noodle-bar concept, serving meat and vegetarian dishes from across Asia and beers from Poland, Mexico and Japan. ⓐ 4–5 South Main St ☎ (021) 427 8874 ⓦ www.wagamama.ie ⏱ 12.30–22.00 Mon–Thur, 12.30–23.00 Fri–Sat, 13.00–22.00 Sun

Café Paradiso ££ ⓫ Highly acclaimed vegetarian restaurant – fulsome reviews on the website make this the best non-meat restaurant anywhere in Ireland. Book in advance to be sure of a table. Recipe books by the chefs can also be purchased. ⓐ 16 Lancaster Quay ☎ (021) 427 7939 ⓦ www.cafeparadiso.ie ⏱ 12.00–15.00, 18.30–22.30 Tues–Sat, closed Sun & Mon

The Weir Bistro & Bar ££ ⑫ Set in the River Lee Hotel, this is rather more than the typical hotel restaurant. The views across the wooded banks of the river are beautiful and the outdoor terrace makes summer evenings a pleasure. Children are catered for and there's a snack menu if you're only after a quick bite. ⓐ The River Lee Hotel, Western Rd ① (021) 425 2700 🕒 07.30–22.00 daily

Fenn's Quay ££–£££ ⑬ Order before 19.30 and a three-course evening meal hovers at the top of the mid-range price category; any later and it is in the higher price range. Expect quality meat dishes – lamb chump kebab with hummus, chargrilled steaks and the like. ⓐ 5 Sheares St ① (021) 427 9527 🕒 08.00–22.00 Mon–Sat, closed Sun

PUBS

An Spailpín Fanach Nooks and crannies, stone floor, a welcoming coal fire when it's cold and a cosy atmosphere make An Spailpín Fanach ('the migrant labourer') very popular at night, especially when there is live music. Ideal for a quiet afternoon drink or a sociable night out. ⓐ 28–29 South Main St ① (021) 427 7949 🕒 12.00–23.30 Mon–Thur, 12.00–00.30 Fri & Sat, 12.30–23.00 Sun

Franciscan Well A microbrewery dishing out Rebel Red, Blarney Blonde, Purgatory Pale Ale and Shandon Stout, all drinks brewed on the premises. There is a spacious beer garden at the back and live music some nights. ⓐ 14 North Mall ① (021) 421 0130 ⓦ www.franciscanwellbrewery.com 🕒 15.00–23.30 Mon–Thur, 15.00–00.30 Fri & Sat, 15.30–23.00 Sun

Reardens Not the place for a quiet drink, especially if there is a hurling or Gaelic football match on the television, this lively and large pub attracts crowds of young punters. Live music on Wednesday, Friday and Sunday nights (check website for details) and an energetic DJ-driven session on Saturday. There is a related nightclub, Havana Brown, around the back on Hanover Street, and this adds to the pub's appeal as a gathering place. Winner of a brace of Best Music Venue in Ireland awards. ⓐ 26 Washington St ⓣ (021) 427 1969 ⓦ www.reardens.com ⓛ 08.00–late daily

CINEMAS & THEATRES
Gate Cork City Six screens, air-conditioned and fully wheelchair accessible. Tickets can be booked online for the standard fare of Hollywood blockbusters. ⓐ North Main St ⓣ (021) 427 9595 ⓦ www.thegatecork.com

UCC Granary Theatre University College The university's own theatre is always worth checking out to see if something interesting is on at the time of your visit. A small in-the-round space where some very experimental performance art and theatre takes place. It is also often used as a gallery space for Cork-based artists to display their work. Besides music, drama and exhibitions the theatre runs some interesting workshops which might be worth checking out. This is as avant-garde as Cork can get. ⓐ Dyke Parade, Mardyke ⓣ (021) 490 4275 ⓦ www.granary.ie

Around Cork

Moving away from the city, Cork boasts a number of attractions within easy reach of the centre. To the east, Fota Wildlife Park is a major attraction and could be combined with a visit to Cobh (see page 115) because it is on the same railway line. On the northwest side of town, Shandon is a neighbourhood just beyond the city centre and can be reached on foot in less than 15 minutes; it is uphill but there is no useful bus service from the centre. Further to the northwest is Blarney, where the famous castle stands, which has hotels, guesthouses and restaurants. A day trip here from Cork is equally manageable; the last bus back to Cork from Blarney is 23.00. The village of Douglas is also just a bus ride away from the centre; in fact it is virtually a suburb of Cork, with a large shopping centre, a number of decent places for a meal and some high-quality hotels.

SIGHTS & ATTRACTIONS

Blarney Castle

The story goes that a Gaelic lord of Blarney was so clever at coming up with excuses for not complying with English orders (either those of Sir George Carew, the English Lord President of Munster, or of Elizabeth I – the story varies) that his name became a synonym for blather and flattering talk. The connection stuck and became related to a particular stone at the castle of Blarney; now, as the tourist literature puts it, this stone has the power of 'conferring eloquence on all who kiss it'. So, for the instant gift of the gab, make your way up on to the battlements of the castle and lean

BEHIND THE BLARNEY
These are the facts behind the blarney. The castle was the main residence of the McCarthy family, and was built as a tower house, in the 15th century. The principal tower is a four-storey structure and then later a five-storey addition was completed. Due to the long line of machicolations ('murder holes'), the stone structures overhanging the wall tops and the large oriel window, the castle looks suitable film-set material. It was a Cormac McCarthy, residing in the castle in the 17th century, whose loquacious talk gave rise to the present use of the word 'blarney', but the actual origins of the ritual of kissing the stone remain a mystery.

backwards – the stone is inside the wall – and with the aid of railings and the help of an assistant you can kiss the magic stone. It is a 26 m (85 ft) drop but there is no danger. You will be photographed kissing the stone and the picture can be purchased. Or you can save your money for the shillelagh keyrings and T-shirts in the souvenir shop. ⓐ 8 km (5 miles) northwest of Cork ⓘ (021) 438 5252 ⓦ www.blarneycastle.ie ⓛ 09.00–18.30 Mon–Sat, 09.00–17.30 Sun (Apr–Oct); 09.00–16.30 daily (Nov–Mar) ⓝ Bus: 224 runs from Parnell Place in Cork ⓘ Admission charge

Blarney Village
You could mistake this neat little village for somewhere in the English countryside: it is certainly not typically Irish, being laid

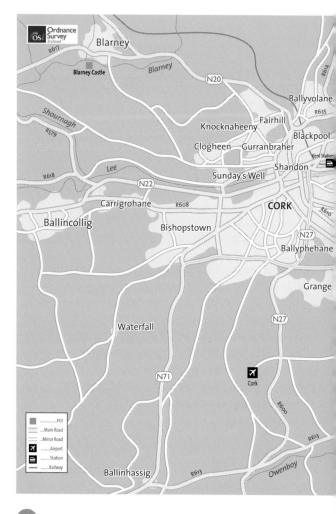

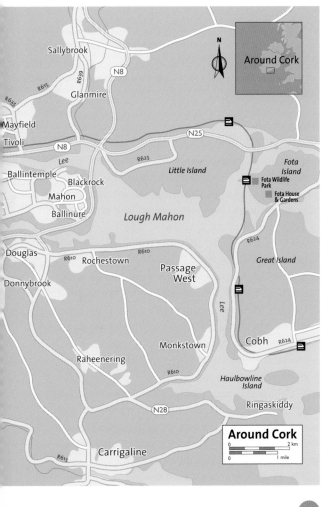

out by General Sir James Jeffreys in the 18th century. The village green is perfect for a picnic, although there are plenty of places to eat indoors as well and there is a small tourist information office to be found here, opening only in the summer. ① Tourist information office: (021) 438 1624 Ⓝ Bus: 224 runs from Parnell Place in Cork

Douglas Village

A trip to Douglas is mainly worthwhile if you are staying or dining at the Maryborough Hotel just outside the village, although both local shopping complexes have large supermarkets and a range of modern shops, and there are some decent restaurants in the village itself. ⓐ Douglas, Cork Ⓝ Bus: 6 from South Mall in Cork

Fota Wildlife Park

Fota Wildlife Park comprises some 28 hectares (70 acres) of open countryside and is situated 16 km (10 miles) east of Cork city. Notwithstanding the steep admission charge (around €13 for adults and €8.50 for children), the park is a non-profit-making concern. Giraffes, flamingos, lemurs, peacocks, kangaroos, rhinos, cheetahs, ostriches and monkeys (including the white-handed gibbon) wander the grounds. It is safe to walk around the signposted trail or, for an extra charge, you can take the tour train that trundles through the park. There is a self-service restaurant and a picnic area. ⓐ Carrigtwohill ① (021) 481 2678 Ⓦ www.fotawildlife.ie Ⓛ 10.00–18.00 Mon–Sat, 11.00–18.00 Sun Ⓝ Train from Kent Station, Cork to Fota train station ① Admission charge

Shandon, Butter Exchange & Firkin Crane Centre

The Shandon area, which retains the narrow streets and vernacular architecture of times gone by, has two unique buildings worth appreciating. The one with the grand Doric-style pillars is the Butter Exchange, built in 1730, where the butter was weighed and checked. The round building that also

🔺 *The Butter Exchange*

occupies the cobbled square was where the butter was bought and sold and it is now the Firkin Crane Centre, where occasional cultural shows take place. ⓐ O'Connell Sq, Shandon

Shandon, St Anne's Church

The church, standing at the top of Shandon hill, is one of the very few landmarks that rises above the city skyline. St Anne's was built in 1722 to replace an earlier church that had burnt down in the 1690 siege of Cork. Two sides of its tower, the north and east ones, are built of red sandstone, while the other two sides are made of limestone. The clock at the top of the tower, known as the 'four-faced liar' because two of its sides tell slightly different times, is surmounted by a 5 m- (16 ft-) long figure of a golden salmon. The inscription at the top of the tower reads: 'Passenger, measure your time, for time is the measure of your being'.

The church interior is nothing special, but a climb to the top of the steeple walls brings you out on a parapet with 360° views of the city. Best of all, you can play the eight bells in the steeple: cards marking out tunes on the numbered bell-ropes make it an easy and fun activity. ⓐ Church St, Shandon ⓣ (021) 450 5906 ⓦ www.shandonbells.org ⓛ 10.00–16.00 Mon–Sat, 11.30–15.30 Sun (Mar–Sept); closed Oct–Feb ⓘ Admission charge

CULTURE

Cork Butter Museum

The importance of butter in Irish life and the economic value of Cork's trade in butter is the subject of this small but highly

◆ St Anne's church tower

focused museum. The story starts in very early times when freshly churned butter was stored in bogs as a means of preserving it, a fact attested to by the occasional finds of ancient wooden barrels, placed in peat centuries ago and lost or forgotten about until discovered by farmers out cutting turf. Cork's importance as a trading centre for butter arose in the 18th century because it could be shipped easily across the Atlantic from the harbour. The butter was brought to the city from the west of the county and Shandon became the main market for buyers and sellers. The museum has a limited number of exhibits but there is plenty to read on the display panels and an audiovisual presentation brings the story up to date. ⓐ O'Connell Sq, Shandon ❶ (021) 430 0600 ⓦ www.corkbutter.museum ❶ 10.00–17.00 daily (Mar–June, Sept & Oct); 10.00–18.00 daily (July & Aug); off season by arrangement ❶ Admission charge

Fota House & Gardens

An 18th-century mansion exhibiting all the opulence and grandeur of Regency-period architecture, with the original plasterwork decorating the ceilings in the main rooms. The butler's servery and kitchens, the servants' quarters, and the scagliola marble in the entrance hall are all highlights of a visit, and the tour is a self-guided one so you can linger where you want to. Screens are accessible in various parts of the house, giving useful social background information. There is also a film looking at cooking in the 19th century. The tearooms, once the billiards room, serve tasty home-made goodies. Entrance to the gardens is free and they are rather magnificent, bearing all the marks of the 19th-century passion for landscaping with exotica. ⓐ Carrigtwohill ⓣ (021) 481 5543 ⓦ www.fotahouse.com ⓛ 10.00–17.00 Mon–Sat, 11.00–17.00 Sun (summer); 11.00–16.00 daily (winter) ⓝ Train from Kent Station, Cork to Fota train station ⓘ Admission charge

RETAIL THERAPY

Blarney Woollen Mills This is a huge store, occupying the premises of what were woollen mills, and alongside the kitsch and gewgaws there is much by way of quality products made in Ireland. Waterford crystal, Carraig Donn knitwear, Mullingar pewter and jewellery are all available here. The website has a full catalogue and online purchases; shipping worldwide is available. ⓐ Village Sq, Blarney ⓣ (021) 451 6111 ⓦ www.blarney.com ⓛ 09.30–18.00 Mon–Sat, 10.00–18.00 Sun

Exchange Toffee Works A few metres down from the Firkin Crane Centre, this is a neat little factory making hard-boiled sweets. You cannot see the candy being manufactured, but what is made here is available for sale. It is not only children who come here for bags of their favourite sweets. ⓐ 37A John Redmond St, Shandon ⓣ (021) 450 7791 ⓛ 09.00–18.00 Mon–Fri, closed Sat & Sun

TAKING A BREAK

Johnny's £ Johnny's bar at Blarney Castle Hotel is attractively placed, overlooking the village green, and the interior retains features of the original building that date back to the 1830s. The tiling is Victorian and the open fire is a welcoming sight on a chilly day. ⓐ Blarney Castle Hotel ⓣ (021) 438 5116 ⓦ www.blarneycastlehotel.com ⓛ 10.30–23.30 Mon–Thur, 10.30–00.30 Fri & Sat, 10.30–23.00 Sun

The Muskerry Arms Bar & Restaurant £ Situated by the village green, this comfortable bar is always good for a cold drink, and there is a restaurant as well as standard pub food. ⓐ Blarney ⓣ (021) 438 5066 ⓦ www.muskerryarms.com ⓛ 07.00–23.00 Mon–Thur, 07.00–00.30 Fri & Sat, 12.30–23.00 Sun

The East Village Bar £–££ Bright and breezy hotel bar and affordable restaurant serving all-day bar food, evening dinner menu, children's menu, special offers on drinks and music in the evenings. Nice place for a quick coffee and dessert or to spend the evening, watching the giant TV screens or listening to live music. ⓐ East Village Douglas ⓣ (021) 736 7000 ⓦ www.eastvillage.ie ⓛ 12.00–23.00 Mon–Fri, all day Sat & Sun

AFTER DARK

Lal Quila £ Of course, not everybody makes their way over to the Emerald Isle in search of a decent curry; but those few who do will strike gold here. You'll get the finest Indian cuisine in the Republic, alongside large portions of outrageous Indo-Irish blarney. Unmissable. ⓐ Old Garda Station, Douglas ⓣ (021) 489 8574 ⓦ www.lalquila.ie ⓛ 12.00–14.30, 17.30–23.30 Mon–Sat, 14.00–22.00 Sun

The Bay Leaf £–££ Inexpensive and very popular, this place has a modern Irish menu, with some unbeatable early-bird offers. Coeliac and child friendly. Light and bright and airy and spacious. ⓐ Main St, Douglas ⓣ (021) 483 5775 ⓦ www.thebayleafdouglas.com ⓛ 12.00–22.00 daily

Four Liars Bistro £–££ The Four Liars Bistro is really the only place in the Shandon area that serves food in the evening. The early-bird menu, served 17.30–19.15, is reasonably good value and includes appetisers such as deep-fried brie and garlic mushrooms and mains of steak and Wiener schnitzel. ⓐ The Butter Exchange, Shandon ⓣ (021) 439 4040 ⓛ 12.00–15.00, 17.00–22.00 Mon–Sat, 12.00–22.00 Sun

Blair's Inn ££ This is the best place to eat in the Blarney area, but it is a ten-minute drive from the village on the R579 road. The food is excellent and can be eaten either in the cosy bar or in one of the dining rooms. There is an attractive riverside garden and live traditional music can be enjoyed on Sunday nights and Mondays during the summer months. ⓐ Cloghroe, Blarney ⓣ (021) 438 1470 ⓦ www.blairsinn.ie ⓛ 12.00–23.30 Mon–Thur, 12.30–00.30 Fri & Sat, 12.30–23.00 Sun; food: 12.30–21.00 daily

Lemon Tree ££ Very different in character to Johnny's bar (see pages 97–8), this is a contemporary-style restaurant serving meat and fish dishes for lunch and dinner. ⓐ Blarney Castle Hotel ⓣ (021) 438 5116 ⓦ www.blarneycastlehotel.com ⓛ 12.00–16.00, 18.30–21.30 daily

Nakon Thai Restaurant ££ No throat-burning Thai chillies but otherwise traditional dishes with tastes of coriander and lime. The desserts are a little disappointing, but at least the beer is from Thailand. **ⓐ** Tramway House, Douglas **ⓣ** (021) 436 9900 **ⓛ** 17.30–23.00 Mon–Sat, 17.00–22.00 Sun

Eco Douglas ££–£££ There's something for everyone at this deservedly popular establishment – pizzas, noodles, steaks, satay and mouthwatering desserts. There's even a neat line in herbal brews. **ⓐ** 1–2 Eastville, Douglas **ⓣ** (021) 489 2522 **ⓦ** www.eco.ie **ⓛ** 12.00–23.00 Mon–Sat, 17.00–23.00 Sun

Flemings £££ Without your own transport, a short taxi ride is required, but the journey is worth making for the comfortable setting and a well-cooked meal in a Georgian family house overlooking the river on the east side of the city. Local ingredients (including black pudding from West Cork), a penchant for French-style sauces and an air of old-fashioned elegance add to the charm of this restaurant and help make it one of the best restaurants in Cork. **ⓐ** Silver Grange House, Tivoli **ⓣ** (021) 482 1621 **ⓦ** www.flemingsrestaurant.ie **ⓛ** 12.00–15.00, 18.30–21.30 daily

ⓓ *Bicycles resting, Kinsale*

OUT OF TOWN

trips

Kinsale

The attractive harbour town of Kinsale (ⓦ http://kinsale.ie), sitting in the mouth of the River Bandon, has built up a reputation for culinary excellence, and there is certainly no shortage of good restaurants. Just wandering its quaintly meandering laneways and discovering tiny, unusual shops makes a visit here worthwhile, although there are many other things to do and see. July provides the lively Kinsale Arts Festival (ⓦ www.kinsaleartsweek.com), October the hyped Gourmet Food festival (ⓦ www.kinsalerestaurants.com) and in summer there is live music somewhere every night. Bike hire, fishing, golf, horse riding, claybird shooting, archery and a variety of watersports are all available nearby. Guided tours and harbour cruises take place in summer: details are displayed at the tourist office (ⓣ (021) 477 2234).

GETTING THERE

Kinsale is 29 km (18 miles) from Cork. Bus Éireann's No 249 service, which takes about 45 minutes, runs daily from the Parnell Place bus station. In summer there are fourteen buses a day during the week (06.40–22.00) and four on Sundays (09.30–18.00). The last bus back to Cork is 22.40 Monday–Saturday and 19.00 on Sunday. **Easy Tours** (ⓣ (021) 454 5328 ⓦ www.easytourscork.com) runs a Kinsale & Atlantic Coast coach trip each Tuesday and Friday.

SPORTS AND WALKS IN KINSALE

The **Oysterhaven Centre** (☎ (021) 477 0738
Ⓦ www.oysterhaven.com) is located on the coast a fair
way outside of Kinsale, so, if you are without a car and
would like to actually have some energy when you get
there, you would need a taxi for transport. Once there,
a range of sports is available – windsurfing, dinghies,
kayaks and a tennis court for hire.

Heritage walks around the town depart from the
tourist office at 10.30 and 16.00 (☎ (021) 477 2729
Ⓦ www.kinsaleheritage.com), and there is also a Historical
Stroll in Old Kinsale that departs from the tourist office at
11.15 (for which call ☎ (021) 477 2873). At night, a Ghost Tour
departs from the Tap Tavern pub at 21.00 (☎ (021) 477 2263
or 0879 480910 for details).

SIGHTS & ATTRACTIONS

Charles Fort

A very well-preserved 17th-century fort that looks most
impressive with its two bastions looking out to sea. The guided
tours, included in the cost of admission, are informative and
interesting. ⓐ Outside town centre, beyond Summercove, but
walkable and signposted ☎ (021) 477 2263 Ⓦ www.opw.ie
🕙 10.00–18.00 daily (mid-Mar–Oct); 10.00–18.00 Sat & Sun
(Nov–mid-Mar) ❶ Admission charge

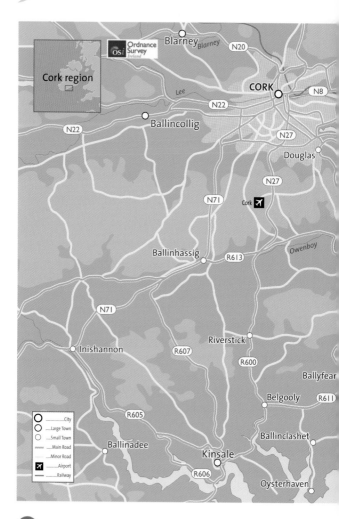

Sallybrook

Dungourney

N8

N25

Midleton

N25

Carrigtohill

Little Island

Lough Mahon

R610

Lee

Passage
West

R624

Great Island

R630

Cloyne

Cobh

Monkstown

Cork Harbour

N28

Aghada

Ringaskiddy

Whitegate

Carrigaline

Power Head

Minane
Bridge

Celtic Sea

N

Cork region

0   4 km

0   2 miles

Kinsale town

The town is picturesque and enjoyable to wander around, checking out the countless restaurants and numerous bars plus some quality craft shops. Tuesday is a good day to visit in the summer because a farmers' market takes place from 09.30 to 13.30 and there are various stalls selling local produce and crafts. For a short walk outside the town, with picnic possibilities, take the signposted road to Scilly and continue on to Charles Fort.

CULTURE

Desmond Castle & the International Museum of Wine

The castle was built around 1500 and two centuries later became a prison. It is now given over to a wine museum, focusing on the fact that some of the Irish nobles who fled to France to escape English rule entered the wine trade on the Continent and made new lives for themselves. ⓐ Cork St ⓣ (021) 477 4855 ⓛ 10.00–17.15 daily (Apr–Oct), closed Sun until mid-June; closed Nov–Mar ⓘ Admission charge

Old Courthouse & Museum

The Courthouse, which dates back to the early 17th century, was used in 1915 for the inquest into the loss of life following the sinking of the British RMS *Lusitania* off the Old Head of Kinsale. The building now houses a small but interesting regional museum. ⓐ Market Sq ⓣ (021) 477 7930 ⓛ Usually 10.30–16.30 Wed–Sun, closed Mon & Tues (but check first) ⓘ Admission charge

RETAIL THERAPY

Boland A wide selection of Irish crafts and clothing, ceramics, jewellery, souvenirs, limited-edition prints and artworks. ⓐ Corner of Emmet St and Pearse St ⓣ (021) 477 2161 ⓦ www.bolandkinsale.com ⓞ 09.00–20.00 Mon–Sat, 10.00–18.30 Sun

Crackpots Pottery If you dine in the brightly coloured restaurant of the same name, you will be eating off plates similar to those for sale in the adjoining showroom. ⓐ 3 Cork St ⓣ (021) 477 2847 ⓦ www.crackpots.ie ⓞ 18.00–22.30 Mon–Fri, 12.00–15.00, 18.00–22.30 Sat & Sun

Cronins This large store has a good selection of garments, Belleek pottery from Northern Ireland, Waterford Crystal and even some Irish truffles. ⓐ Corner of Emmet St and Pearse St ⓣ (021) 477 2192 ⓞ 09.30–18.00 Mon–Sat, closed Sun

Enibas Contemporary, Irish-designed silver, gold and platinum jewellery. Most of what you see comes from the Enibas workshop in Schull, West Cork, and was handcrafted by designer Sabine Lenz. ⓐ 42 Main St ⓣ (021) 477 7022 ⓦ www.enibas.com ⓞ 10.00–18.00 Mon–Sat, 11.00–18.00 Sun

Giles Norman Gallery Black-and-white Irish landscape photographs, framed and unframed, with an eye for the wild and rugged beauty of West Cork. ⓐ 45 Main St ⓣ (021) 477 4373 ⓦ www.gilesnorman.com ⓞ 10.00–18.00 Mon–Sat, 12.00–18.00 Sun

Granny's Bottom Drawer Yes! Just what you came here for – selections of lacework. ⓐ 53 Main St ⓣ (021) 477 4839 ⓛ 10.00–20.00 Mon–Sat, closed Sun

Glenaran Stocks unique Irish gifts and specialises in a large variety of knitwear. ⓐ Market St ⓣ (021) 477 3384 ⓦ www.glenaran.com ⓛ 09.30–18.00 daily (June–Sept); 09.30–20.00 daily (Oct–May)

Hilary Hale Working with wood from local trees that have been brought down in storms, Hilary Hale turns out bowls, lamps and platters with simple, elegant forms. ⓐ Rincurran Hall, Summercove ⓣ (021) 477 2010 ⓦ www.hilaryhale.com ⓛ 11.00–17.00 daily (summer) ⓘ It is advisable to phone in advance for an appointment out of season

Kinsale Crystal Locally made crystal only available from this shop; shipping can be arranged. ⓐ 2 Market St ⓣ (021) 477 4493 ⓦ www.kinsalecrystal.ie ⓛ 10.00–17.30 Mon–Sat (all year); 12.00–18.00 Sun (summer only)

Kinsale Pottery & Art School Ceramics, photographs, watercolours, oils, prints, sculpture and stained glass – all by Cork-based artists. To get here, turn left at the White House hotel, go around Market Square to pass St Multose church and up the old Bandon Road to the top of the hill. After 300 m (330 yds), turn left at the signpost. ⓐ Olcote ⓣ (021) 477 7758 ⓦ www.kinsaleceramics.com ⓛ 10.00–18.00 daily

🔵 *Kinsale is home to a number of craft shops*

TAKING A BREAK

Armada Bar £ Good old-fashioned favourites such as beef in Guinness®, Irish stew, chowder, sandwiches and soup – all on tap at this pub. ⓐ 6 Market St ⓣ (021) 477 2255 ⓛ 12.00–20.00 daily (Mar–Nov); closed Dec–Feb

Café Blue £ Great food and coffees, wine, speciality beer, very comfortable surroundings and good service. Hard to beat. ⓐ Blue Haven Hotel, Pearse St ⓣ (021) 477 2209 ⓦ www.bluehavenkinsale.com ⓛ 08.30–17.30 Mon–Fri, 09.00–18.00 Sat & Sun

Cuchina £ Mediterranean-style food, nothing too heavy, at this friendly little eatery. ⓐ 9 Market St ⓣ (021) 470 0707 ⓛ 08.00–17.00 Mon–Sat, closed Sun

Mange Tout £ This good-value eatery is next to the Boland newspaper and craft shop. Drop in for tasty soups, chicken chasseur, spicy beef, real vegetarian choices, quiches, desserts, pastries, ice cream, sorbets and a wide selection of coffees. ⓐ Pearse St ⓣ (021) 470 6899 ⓛ 09.00–18.00 Mon–Fri, 09.00–17.00 Sat, closed Sun

Waterfront Bar & Bistro £–££ Soups, sandwiches, seafood and steaks in a hotel that aspires to poshness. ⓐ Actons Hotel, Pier Rd ⓣ (021) 477 9900 ⓦ www.actonshotelkinsale.com ⓛ 12.00–22.00 daily

◆ *One of Kinsale's culinary highlights*

GOURMET CAPITAL

Kinsale's reputation as the gourmet capital of Ireland is reflected in the Good Food Circle of 12 member restaurants (ⓦ www.kinsalerestaurants.com) and the Kinsale Gourmet Festival, which is held each year in October. The 12 are:

Fishy Fishy Café ££ ⓐ Crowleys Quay ⓣ (021) 470 0415
ⓛ 12.00–21.00 Tues–Sat, 12.00–16.30 Sun & Mon (Mar–Oct)

White Lady Restaurant ££ ⓐ White Lady Hotel, O'Connell St
ⓣ (021) 477 2737 ⓛ 17.00–22.00 Mon–Sat, 13.00–22.00 Sun

blu Restaurant ££–£££ ⓐ Blue Haven Hotel, Pearse St
ⓣ (021) 477 2209 ⓛ 18.00–22.00 daily

Crackpots Restaurant ££–£££ ⓐ 3 Cork St ⓣ (021) 477 2847
ⓛ 12.00–22.00 daily

Jim Edwards Bar & Restaurant ££–£££ ⓐ Market Quay ⓣ (021)
477 2541 ⓛ Bar: 12.30–22.00; restaurant: 18.00–22.00 daily

Man Friday ££–£££ ⓐ Scilly ⓣ (021) 477 2260 ⓛ 18.45–22.00
Mon–Sat, closed Sun

Max's Wine Bar ££–£££ ⓐ 48 Main St ⓣ (021) 477 2443
ⓛ 12.30–13.30, 18.30–22.00 daily (May–mid-Dec), closed
Mon (mid-Mar–May); closed mid-Dec–mid-Mar

Restaurant d'Antibes ££–£££ @ 2 Pearse St ☎ (021) 477 2125
🕐 18.00–22.00 daily

Spinnaker Bar & Restaurant ££–£££ @ Scilly ☎ (021) 477 2098
🕐 18.00–22.00 Tues–Sat, closed Sun & Mon

Captain's Table Restaurant £££ @ Actons Hotel, Pier Rd
☎ (021) 477 9900 🕐 19.00–21.30 daily

Pier One £££ @ Trident Hotel, Worlds End ☎ (021) 477 9300
🕐 19.00–21.30 daily

Toddies Restaurant £££ @ Kinsale Brewery, The Glen
☎ (021) 477 7769 🕐 18.30–22.30 daily

AFTER DARK

Mediterraneo Restaurant £–££ A good-quality, good-value Italian
restaurant. @ 7 Pearse St ☎ (021) 477 3844
🌐 www.mediterraneokinsale.com 🕐 18.00–22.00 daily

Spaniard Bar & Restaurant £–££ Take an evening stroll out to
Scilly, signposted from the centre of town, and enjoy a drink in
this sociable bar while perusing the bar and restaurant
menus: this is one way of relaxing in Kinsale after dark.
@ Scilly ☎ (021) 477 2436 🌐 www.thespaniard.ie
🕐 Bar: 12.00–18.00; restaurant: 18.30–22.00 daily

ACCOMMODATION

Danabel £–££ Less than five minutes on foot from the town centre, this modern house has five en-suite bedrooms with tea- and coffee-making facilities and a lounge. ⓐ Sleaveen, Featherbed Lane ⓣ (021) 477 4087 ⓦ www.danabel.com

Blindgate House ££ Bright and airy, this purpose-built luxury accommodation with its own gardens and off-street parking is within walking distance of the town. ⓐ Blindgate St ⓣ (021) 477 7858 ⓦ www.blindgatehouse.com

Rockview ££ Bedrooms in a quiet location, with good facilities and a very short walk to the town centre. ⓐ The Glen ⓣ (021) 477 3162 ⓦ www.rockviewbb.com

Tierney's Guesthouse ££ Well-established guesthouse in the centre of town, with all the desired facilities. ⓐ 70 Main St ⓣ (021) 477 2205 ⓦ www.tierneys-kinsale.com

Harbour Lodge £££ Classy guesthouse right on the seafront with huge windows and a panoramic view of the harbour. Breakfasts are nice and the restaurant is good. ⓐ Scilly ⓣ (021) 477 2376 ⓦ www.harbourlodge.com

Old Bank House £££ In the centre of town, once an old bank, this comfortable guesthouse has excellent facilities and delicious breakfasts. ⓐ 11 Pearse St ⓣ (021) 477 4075 ⓦ www.oldbankhousekinsale.com

Cobh & Midleton

The small but historically important town of Cobh is pronounced 'cove' and was called Queenstown, after the British queen, Victoria, between 1849 and Irish independence in 1922. If you take a boat from Cork, you see and leave Cobh behind from the water, as did many hundreds of thousands of emigrants who left for America in the 19th and early 20th centuries. Queenstown was also the last port of call for the *Titanic*. Today, Cobh is a pleasant and lively coastal town that benefits from an injection of English vernacular architecture, making the town resemble a seaside resort on England's southern coast, but characteristically Irish at the same time. The town lacks a beach but boasts an excellent museum and is well worth a day trip from Cork city.

Midleton is an inland town, lying to the east of Cork city. While noteworthy for one major museum, it also benefits from an excellent restaurant. Both Cobh and Midleton are easy to get to in a day and Cobh is also a place where you might be tempted to stay a night.

GETTING THERE

Cobh is 24 km (15 miles) southeast of Cork and is situated on an island (see map on pages 104–5). Trains, mostly ones coming into Cork from Mallow in the north of the county, stop at Cork's Kent Station (☎ (021) 450 6766) before continuing on to Cobh, taking just under half an hour. There are over a dozen trains a day, Monday to Saturday, starting at 07.30 and leaving on the hour from 09.00 to 18.00, with the last train going at 20.30.

⬥ *Statue of emigrants at the heritage centre*

BEAUTY AND THE BEASTS

Cork–Cobh trains also stop at Fota, so it is possible to visit Fota Wildlife Park and Fota House & Gardens (see pages 92 and 96–7) as part of a trip to or from Cobh. If you started early in the morning, both Fota and Cobh could be taken in on one busy day, though there are good accommodation possibilities that make an overnight stay worth considering.

On Sunday trains depart at 08.45 and 11.45, with four in the afternoon and the last one leaving at 21.50. The last train back from Cobh to Cork is at 23.00 Monday to Saturday and 22.25 on Sunday.

Midleton is 24 km (15 miles) east of Cork and buses 241 and 261 depart from Parnell Place in Cork (☎ (021) 450 8188). There are around 20 buses a day Monday to Saturday, taking 20 minutes. The last bus back to Cork from Midleton is at 22.15. No services run, though, on 25 or 26 December.

COBH

SIGHTS & ATTRACTIONS

There is a **tourist office** (☎ (021) 481 3301 ⏱ 09.30–17.30 Mon–Fri, 13.00–17.00 Sat & Sun (summer); 09.30–17.30 Mon–Fri, closed Sat & Sun (winter)), in the centre of town, a five-minute walk from the train station, dispensing free town maps. To learn more about the town's *Titanic* links, embark on a Titanic Trail walk. ☎ (021) 481 5211 ⓦ www.titanic-trail.com ⏱ 11.00, 14.00 daily (June–Aug); 11.00 daily (Mar–May & Sept); Oct–Feb, telephone for tour timings

Town walk

From the train station walk towards town. Opposite the heritage centre, walk up Spy Hill to high ground looking down on the town and harbour. The nearest visible island is Haulbowline, while the greener island nearer to the mouth of the harbour is Spike Island. The British built a fort on Spike Island, later used to hold prisoners awaiting transportation to Australia, and the Irish used the island as a prison until 2004. Take the left turning, Bishop's Road, and turn right at the top to walk towards St Colman's Cathedral. Designed by E W Pugin and G C Ashli, the building of the neo-Gothic cathedral took from 1860 to 1915, and you can judge for yourself whether the final result is an attraction or an aberration. Either way, there are splendid views from outside the cathedral. Walk down towards the town centre, via Cathedral Place and Harbour Hill, and you will come out on East beach near the town hall. It is a five-minute walk from here back to the town centre.

CULTURE

Cobh Museum

What was a Presbyterian church dating back to the mid-19th century is now a small museum covering local history, with a natural emphasis on matters maritime. ⓐ Scot's church, High Rd ⓣ (021) 481 4240 ⓦ www.cobhmuseum.com ⓛ 11.00–13.00, 14.00–17.30 Mon–Sat, 15.00–18.00 Sun (Apr–Oct); closed Nov–Mar ⓘ Admission charge

Cobh, The Queenstown Story

The town's rich but melancholy history is told in this interesting and very popular heritage centre. Cobh's port was one of Ireland's most important departure points for emigrants seeking a better life across the Atlantic, and vessels carrying convicts to Australia also departed from here. Queenstown was also the last port of call for the *Lusitania* before the ship sank off the coast near Kinsale. Many of the *Lusitania*'s victims were brought into Cobh and buried in the cemetery outside of town. ❷ Old Railway Station ❶ (021) 481 3591 ⓦ www.cobhheritage.com ❸ 09.30–17.00 Mon–Sat, 11.00–17.00 Sun; open later in summer ❶ Admission charge

TAKING A BREAK

Between the railway station and the town centre there is a promenade and a small gardened area looking out to sea. A picnic could be enjoyed here with provisions bought from the supermarket on the other side of the road or, next to the supermarket, a takeaway from the River Room café. The heritage centre also has a café serving meals and snacks, but in the summer the place is heaving with people and is hardly the best place to take a break and relax.

O'Shea's £ The grand-looking Commodore Hotel is hard to miss, a little way past the heritage centre and on your left when walking into town from the railway station. The comfortable and popular bar serves food at lunchtime (in winter this becomes a carvery). ❷ Commodore Hotel, Westbourne Place ❶ (021) 481 1277 ❸ 10.30–15.00, 17.00–18.45 daily

The Roaring Donkey £ An old-fashioned (in the good sense) pub with traditional live music on Wednesday nights. ❷ Top O' the Hill ❶ (021) 481 1739 ❸ 11.30–23.30 daily

The Water's Edge Hotel Bar & Restaurant (Jacob's Ladder) £
Sandwiches and pastries or, for a more substantial lunch,
a Hereford beefburger in a floury bap. ⓐ Next to Cobh, The
Queenstown Story ⓣ (021) 481 5566 ⓦ www.watersedgehotel.ie
ⓛ 12.00–16.00 daily

Tradewinds ££–£££ Bar food, snacks and a very good restaurant
whose allure is magnified by the relaxed and welcoming
atmosphere. ⓐ 16 Casement Sq ⓣ (021) 481 3754
ⓛ 12.00–15.00, 18.00–22.30 Mon–Sat, closed Sun

AFTER DARK
Jacob's Ladder Restaurant ££–£££ Jacob's has the reputation
as the best place to eat in Cobh and it is certainly the most
stylish place to enjoy an evening meal in town. The seafood
is the main draw, but meat dishes are also available; reserve
a table by the windows for harbour views. ⓐ Water's Edge
Hotel, next to Cobh, The Queenstown Story ⓣ (021) 481 5566
ⓦ www.watersedgehotel.ie ⓛ 18.00–21.00 daily

ACCOMMODATION
Amberleigh House ££ A couple of minutes from the town
centre, a Victorian-era house that would not be out of place in
an English seaside resort, with views of the town down below.
ⓐ West End Terrace ⓣ (021) 481 4069 ⓦ www.amberleigh.ie

Radisson Blu ££–£££ If planning an overnight stay to facilitate
visits to Fota and Cobh, the Radisson is handily situated within
walking distance of Little Island station on the Cork–Cobh railway

◆ *A bar in Cobh commemorates the RMS* Lusitania

line that also stops at Fota. Good facilities, restaurant, bar and a terrific spa. ⓐ Little Island ⓣ (021) 429 7000 ⓦ www.radissonblu.ie

Knockeven House £££ An 1840s period house, a little way outside of the town centre but walkable, with large rooms. ⓐ Rushbrooke ⓣ (021) 481 1778 ⓦ www.knockevenhouse.com

MIDLETON

Home to the famous Jameson Irish whiskey, Midleton is worth visiting in order to tour the Jameson Experience and enjoy a meal or drink in this typical Cork market town. There is also an interesting craft centre in the town centre, selling handmade items. If your visit takes place on a Saturday, there is a lively farmers' market (ⓛ 09.00–14.00) behind the courthouse on Main Street. Midleton's tourist office is right next to the Old Midleton Distillery (ⓣ (021) 461 3702 ⓛ 09.15–13.00, 14.00–17.00 Mon–Sat, closed Sun (June–Sept); closed Oct–May) and you can collect a free town map here as well as make use of the booking service for accommodation in the area.

CULTURE
Jameson Experience
The first part of your visit, a short film about the distillery, is the least engaging element of this otherwise excellent tour, especially if every cell in your body is screaming out for a drop of the hard stuff. It starts out in the yard where farmers once delivered the barley that makes the whole thing interesting

and then conducts you around the production process, explaining how the whiskey is distilled. There is some terrific machinery still in place and, at the tour's end, the thing you really came for – a free taste of the whiskey in the bar (where further drinks can be purchased and new friends made). ⓐ Distillery Rd ☎ (021) 461 3594 ⓦ www.jamesonwhiskey.com 🕐 10.00–18.00 (last tour at 16.30) daily (Mar–Oct); tours: 11.30, 14.30, 16.00 daily (Nov–Feb) ⓘ Admission charge

RETAIL THERAPY

Silverstone Dimensions Silver and gold jewellery, designed and handmade on the premises by Shmuel Yolzari, and distinguished by the incorporation of ebony into the pieces. ⓐ The Courtyard, 8 Main St ☎ (021) 463 4758 ⓦ www.sdyolzari.com 🕐 09.30–17.00 Mon–Sat, closed Sun

TAKING A BREAK

Farmgate £ As with Farmgate in the English Market in Cork (see pages 67 and 69), you can expect lovely food using local produce. The hot food stops at 16.00, but drinks and cakes are available for another hour. Farmgate is a short walk away from the distillery off the west end of Main Street. ⓐ Coolbawn ☎ (021) 463 2771 🕐 09.00–17.30 Mon–Wed, 09.00–17.00 Thur & Fri, closed Sat & Sun

Malt House Restaurant £ This is the most convenient place for a light meal or drink when visiting the distillery. Expect shepherd's pie, lasagne, salads, cakes and the like. ⓐ Distillery Rd ☎ (021) 461 3594 ⓦ www.jamesonwhiskey.com 🕐 10.00–17.00 daily

AFTER DARK

Farmgate ££ Traditional pine furniture stands alongside modern touches in this rather wonderful restaurant, which undergoes a transformation from daytime café to sophisticated evening venue. It has restricted opening hours and a reservation is all the more necessary because of this. ⓐ Coolbawn
ⓣ (021) 463 2771 ⓛ 18.30–21.30 Thur–Sat, closed Sun–Wed

ACCOMMODATION

An Stór Hostel £ A converted mill, this hostel is fine for a one-night stay and there are private doubles and family rooms as well as dorm beds. ⓐ Drury's Ave, off Main St ⓣ (021) 463 3106
ⓦ www.anstor.com

Midleton Park Hotel £££ Child friendly, spa and leisure centre, good restaurant, traditional music at weekends. ⓐ Old Cork Rd
ⓣ (021) 463 5100 ⓦ www.midletonpark.com

ⓓ *Don't lose your bearings*

PRACTICAL
information

Directory

GETTING THERE
By air

There are direct flights from cities in the UK – just over an hour from London – and from continental Europe, as well as from Dublin, Galway and Belfast. The main airlines operating from the UK are Aer Lingus (Heathrow), easyJet (Gatwick), Ryanair (Stansted and Liverpool), Aer Arann (Bristol, Cardiff, Edinburgh, Leeds, Southampton, Newquay), and bmibaby (Birmingham, Durham Tees Valley, Leeds Bradford, Manchester), all with online booking.

Aer Lingus also connects Cork with many European cities, including Amsterdam, Berlin, Madrid, Paris and Prague.

Aer Lingus 0871 718 5000 www.aerlingus.com
easyJet 0871 244 2366 www.easyjet.com
Ryanair 0871 246 0000 www.ryanair.com
Aer Arann 0800 587 2324 www.aerarann.com
bmibaby 0870 264 2229 www.bmibaby.com

Many people are aware that air travel emits CO_2, which contributes to climate change. You may be interested in the possibility of lessening the environmental impact of your flight through the charity **Climate Care** (www.jpmorganclimatecare.com), which offsets your CO_2 by funding environmental projects around the world.

By water

Ferry services operate between Swansea (Wales) and Cork and between Roscoff in France and Cork. The Swansea–Cork ferries operate all year, taking ten hours, and, from April to early October, there are sailings from Roscoff to Cork with Brittany Ferries.

Swansea–Cork Ferries ☎ 0844 576 8831

🌐 www.fastnetline.com

Brittany Ferries ☎ (021) 427 7801 (Ireland)

🌐 www.brittanyferries.ie

By water & rail

Cork has a rail link with Dublin and other cities, and combined rail and ferry tickets from the UK are available.

🌐 www.nationalrail.co.uk and, in Ireland, **Iarnród Éireann** (Irish Rail) 🌐 www.irishrail.ie

By water & road

There is a daily London (Victoria)–Cork coach service, departing London at 19.00 and arriving 11.05 the next day. Book online at 🌐 www.eurolines.co.uk ☎ 08717 818181

ENTRY FORMALITIES

All visitors require a valid passport. EU nationals can stay indefinitely without a visa and travellers from the USA, Canada, Australia and New Zealand can stay three months without a visa. See 🌐 www.foreignaffairs.gov.ie for further details.

There are no customs restrictions or duty-free allowances for EU nationals.

MONEY

Ireland uses the euro, which is divided into 100 cents. Coins are in the denominations of 1, 2, 5, 10, 20 and 50 cents, and of 1 and 2 euros. The denominations for notes are 5, 10, 20, 50, 100, 200 and 500 euros.

ATMs (cash machines) can be found at the airport and outside banks throughout Cork city centre, as well as in Kinsale, Cobh and Midleton; you can withdraw cash from these with a credit card 24 hours a day. Money and traveller's cheques can be exchanged at banks (🕐 10.00–16.00 Mon–Fri). Credit cards are widely accepted in hotels, shops and restaurants.

HEALTH, SAFETY & CRIME

There are no compulsory vaccinations and tap water is safe to drink. Nicotine-stained walls in pubs are history – smoking is no longer allowed in any place where people are employed. Note that the possession of even tiny amounts of cannabis is a crime and will probably involve a court case and a fine. Public drunkenness is also a crime.

TRAVEL INSURANCE

A good policy will cover medical treatment, baggage cover and theft or loss of possessions. You will need to make a police report for non-medical claims and ensure you keep any receipts for medical treatment. Consider keeping a copy of your policy and emergency contact numbers in your email account for easy retrieval.

HEALTH INFORMATION WEBSITES

Ⓦ www.cdc.gov/travel and Ⓦ www.healthfinder.gov for American travellers

Ⓦ www.dh.gov.uk/travellers and Ⓦ www.fco.gov.uk/travel for health and travel advice from the British government

Ⓦ www.travelhealth.co.uk for useful tips and information

Ⓦ www.tripprep.com Travel Health Online

Ⓦ www.who.int/en World Health Organization

EU travellers on holiday are entitled to free medical treatment, but you will need your European Health Insurance Card (EHIC), which can be obtained by British nationals from Ⓦ www.ehic.org.uk. However, this does not cover repatriation or long-term illness, so visitors should get cover for these eventualities as well. Non-EU visitors should also have travel insurance arranged beforehand to cover medical emergencies. A visit to a GP will entail a consultation fee of €50–60, including prescription. The cost of prescriptive medicines may vary from €10 to €30. These fees are not refundable. Contraception is available over the counter in Ireland, but the morning-after pill can only be obtained on prescription.

Cork is safer than most major European cities, but common sense dictates being careful as regards personal possessions and safety. While it is safe to walk around city-centre streets until late into the evening, be aware that you may come across drunken louts after the bars close. Members of the unarmed police force, called the Garda, wear navy-blue uniforms and travel in blue and white cars labelled Garda Síochána.

Have a list of the numbers of any traveller's cheques and keep this with your proof of purchase (which will be needed for a claim) and the contact number to use in case the cheques are lost or stolen. Keep this information separate from the cheques themselves; posting them to an email account is a good idea. Keep a photocopy of the main page of your passport and, if applicable, the page with the stamp of your visa, and keep these separate from your passport. Consider keeping the number of your passport, or a scanned copy of the relevant pages, in an email that can be retrieved if necessary.

You should make a note before you travel of the number to ring in the event of a lost or stolen credit card. An incident report should be collected for insurance purposes. The main police station, **Garda Síochána**, is in Anglesea Street (🕿 (021) 452 2000). See page 136, Emergencies, for contact telephone numbers.

OPENING HOURS

Shops and offices generally tend to open from 09.00 or 09.30 to 17.30 Monday to Saturday, with many of the city-centre stores staying open until 20.00 on Thursdays and from 13.00 to 17.00 on Sundays. For banking hours see the Money section on page 128. Hours for museums and attractions vary, with opening times at 09.00, 09.30 or even later and closing times usually between 17.00 and 18.00.

TOILETS

There are toilets at the bus station and department stores and, for customers' use, in restaurants and bars. Toilets are usually marked on the doors by the international symbols for men and women, but might occasionally be marked *fir* for men and *mná* for women. The general standard of public toilets is variable.

CHILDREN

Parks offer open space for children to spread their wings, and Fota Wildlife Park (see page 92) will delight the whole family. Fitzgerald Park (see page 74) has a fantastic playground as well, mainly aimed at younger ones. The grislier elements of Cork City Gaol (see page 79) should also appeal to children, as will the chance to make a racket by ringing the bells at the Shandon

🔺 *Comfortable coach rides*

church (see page 94). The Oysterhaven Centre in Kinsale (see page 103) offers water-based activities for older children. The Queenstown Story heritage centre (see pages 118–19), in Cobh, should engage the little ones' interest.

Cork is generally a child-friendly place and there should be no problems in hotels and restaurants. Finding suitable food should not be difficult either, and children's menus are common. Baby food and nappies are readily available in supermarkets.

The intriguingly named **Chuckie's** (ⓐ Doughcloyne Industrial Estate, Sarsfield Rd, Wilton ⓣ (021) 434 4112 ⓦ www.chuckies.ie) is an indoor adventure play centre with various activities and a toddler area for under-fives. Admission for adults, who must accompany their children, is free, and the cost is around €7.50 for each child. Older children with an interest in the way things work will love **Lifetime Lab** (ⓐ Lee Rd ⓣ (021) 494 1500 ⓦ www.lifetimelab.ie). The buildings and machinery of the city's old waterworks, well preserved and opened to the public, are ideal for children – there are interactive bits and pieces, a steam centre, playground, picnic area and – for the adults – restful views over the River Lee.

COMMUNICATIONS

Internet

Most hotels and hostels have Internet access for guests, and there are Internet cafés located around the city. **Web Workhouse**, on one of the streets connecting Patrick Street with Oliver Plunkett Street, is open 24 hours every day of the year.
ⓐ 8A Winthrop St ⓣ (021) 427 3090 ⓦ www.webworkhouse.com
Internet Café ⓐ 10 Paul St ⓣ (021) 485 1546 ⓛ 08.00–23.00 daily

Phone

Public phones in Ireland take both coins and prepaid phonecards, and some take credit cards. Prepaid phonecards are available from newsagents. Beware of using the phone in your hotel room without first checking the rates. Cork phone numbers have seven digits. If you are calling from outside the city, you must add the area code, which is 021.

Dial 11811 for telephone directory enquiries for numbers within Ireland and Northern Ireland. When dialling a number in Northern Ireland, dial 048 followed by the area code minus the 0 and then the number.

TELEPHONING IRELAND

Dial the international access code for the country you are in, followed by the international country code for Ireland, which is 353, followed by the Cork city code, which is 021, minus the 0. To telephone, for example, (021) 123 4567 from the UK you would dial 00+353+21+123 4567.

TELEPHONING ABROAD

Dial 00, the international access code, followed by the country code of the country you are telephoning and then the area code minus the initial zero, followed by the number itself. To telephone, for example, 0207 123 4567 in the UK from Ireland you would dial 00+44+207+123 4567.

Australia: 61	Germany: 49	Spain: 34
Canada: 1	New Zealand: 64	UK: 44
France: 33	South Africa: 27	USA: 1

For national operator assistance dial 10, and for international operator assistance dial 114. For pricing information see
Ⓦ www.eircom.ie

Your mobile phone should work in Ireland, though check with your provider if you are unsure. As with hotel phones, check the rates, and be aware of charges for receiving calls from abroad.

Post

The main post office is in Oliver Plunkett Street (Ⓣ (021) 485 1032), and there are sub post offices in MacCurtain Street, Washington Street and North Main Street. A letter not over 50g or a postcard to a destination in Ireland or Northern Ireland is 55 cents, and the same letter or postcard to Britain or the rest of the world costs slightly more. Letters abroad can be registered for around €5, with the recipient signing for them, and a courier service is also available through the post office. See
Ⓦ www.anpost.ie for the full range of postal services.

ELECTRICITY

The electricity supply is 220–40 volts, 50 Hertz. Plugs have three square pins as in the UK. Adapters for US and European appliances can be bought at the airport and from electrical shops around the city. See Ⓦ www.kropla.com for more information.

TRAVELLERS WITH DISABILITIES

Wheelchair access is becoming more prevalent and some hotels have wheelchair-friendly rooms, but this cannot be taken for granted. Some of the city's sights are inaccessible to wheelchair users. Contact the **Irish Wheelchair Association** (Ⓣ 01 8186 400

ⓦ www.iwa.ie) for more detailed information. Before booking your flight, check with the airlines about the facilities they can offer at Cork airport. A guide to international airlines and the facilities and services they provide for passengers with disabilities can be found at ⓦ www.allgohere.com

TOURIST INFORMATION

Cork's tourist office is located on Grand Parade. ☎ 425 5100
ⓦ www.corkkerry.ie ⏰ 09.00–19.00 Mon–Sat, 09.00–15.00 Sun (July & Aug); 09.30–17.30 Mon–Sat, closed Sun (Sept–June)

Websites

ⓦ www.tourismireland.com
Australia ⓦ www.tourismireland.com
USA ⓦ www.discoverireland.com/us

BACKGROUND READING

The Burning of Cork by Gerry White and Brendan O'Shea. Fascinating and engrossing historical account of the background to the night in 1920 when British forces delivered an unequivocal answer to Irish guerrilla activities: they set fire to the city.

Emergencies

The following are the national emergency numbers. For fire, police or an ambulance dial ☎ 999 or 112 and tell the operator which service you require.

MEDICAL SERVICES

In a medical emergency your place of accommodation should be able to supply a contact for a local GP, or you can go to the Accident and Emergency (A&E) department at **Cork University Hospital** (📍 Wilton ☎ (021) 454 6400) or **Cork South Infirmary Victoria Hospital** (📍 Old Blackrock Rd ☎ (021) 492 6100). A centrally located doctor's clinic is **Dr Der Moloney** (📍 9 Patrick St ☎ (021) 427 8699 🕐 10.00–14.00, 16.00–18.00 Mon & Fri, 09.30–19.00 Tues & Thur, 10.00–14.00, 16.00–19.00 Wed, closed Sat & Sun).

There is a dental school at **Cork University Hospital** (☎ (021) 490 1100 🕐 09.00–17.00 Mon–Fri, closed Sat & Sun) and a 24-hour emergency dental service at the hospital's A&E department. A private dental clinic, closer to the city centre, is **Thos. E Callaghan** (📍 17 South Mall ☎ (021) 427 1097 🕐 09.00–19.00 Mon–Fri, 09.30–18.00 Sat, closed Sun).

Phelans Regional Late Night Pharmacy in the Wilton Centre opposite Cork University Hospital (☎ (021) 434 4575) is open daily until 22.00.

POLICE

The main Cork Garda (police) station is situated on Anglesea Street (☎ (021) 452 2000).

EMBASSIES & CONSULATES

Embassies and consular offices are mostly located in Dublin:
Australia ☎ 01 6645 300; Britain ☎ 01 2053 700; New Zealand
☎ 01 6604 233; South Africa ☎ 01 6615 553; USA ☎ 01 6688 777

🔺 *The attractive harbour at Cobh*

ACKNOWLEDGEMENTS

The publishers would like to thank the following individuals and organisations for supplying their copyright photographs for this book: Cork City Gaol, pages 42–3; Dreamstime, page 13 (Judith Picciotto), page 20 (Canettistock), page 21 (Michael Walsh); iStockphoto.com, page 125 (jorgene); Rainer Ebert, pages 25 & 65; robcheo2, page 8; Sean Sheehan, all others.

Project editor: Kate Taylor
Layout: Donna Pedley
Proofreaders: Karolin Thomas & Jan McCann

Send your thoughts to
books@thomascook.com

- Found a great bar, club, shop or must-see sight that we don't feature?
- Like to tip us off about any information that needs a little updating?
- Want to tell us what you love about this handy little guidebook and more importantly how we can make it even handier?

Then here's your chance to tell all! Send us ideas, discoveries and recommendations today and then look out for your valuable input in the next edition of this title.

Email the above address (stating the title) or write to:
pocket guides Series Editor, Thomas Cook Publishing, PO Box 227, Coningsby Road, Peterborough PE3 8SB, UK.

WHAT'S IN YOUR GUIDEBOOK?

WHAT'S IN YOUR GUIDEBOOK?

Independent authors Impartial up-to-date information from our travel experts who meticulously source local knowledge.

Experience Thomas Cook's 165 years in the travel industry and guidebook publishing enriches every word with expertise you can trust.

Travel know-how Thomas Cook has thousands of staff working around the globe, all living and breathing travel.

Editors Travel-publishing professionals, pulling everything together to craft a perfect blend of words, pictures, maps and design.

You, the traveller We deliver a practical, no-nonsense approach to information, geared to how you really use it.